Solving the Grading Puzzle for Students with Disabilities

Dennis D. Munk
Northern Illinois University

KNOWLEDGE

by Design, Inc.

Whitefish Bay, Wisconsin

KNOWLEDGE
by Design, Inc.

Knowledge by Design, Inc.
5907 N. Kent Avenue
Whitefish Bay, WI 53217

Solving the Grading Puzzle for Students with Disabilities
Copyright © 2003 by Dennis D. Munk.

Cover Art: Jennifer Cooney Vulpas
Cover Design: Kari Moyle
Copy Editor: Kirstin McBride

ISBN 0-9708429-7-x

Printed in the United States of America

Second Printing

Dedication

This book is dedicated to my wife Karen and sons Caleb and Sam for their abundant love, spirit, and support. You gave me a reason to start and to finish.

Acknowledgments

Research described herein was funded by a grant (H324D000062-01) from the U.S. Department of Education, Office of Special Education (CFDA. 84.324D: Directed Research Projects) to Northern Illinois University. Statements should not, however, be interpreted as official policy of the agencies.

Special thanks to Dr. Bill Bursuck, co-investigator (and mentor) on the project. Thanks also to the students, parents, and teachers who have participated in the project and whose ideas have shaped the contents of this book.

Author Biography

Dennis D. Munk Ed.D., is an associate professor in the Department of Teaching & Learning at Northern Illinois University in Dekalb, Illinois, where he teaches undergraduate and graduate courses in the teacher preparation program. He has conducted research in the areas of grading, homework, functional assessment, and feeding disorders, and has 20 years of experience in special education and mental health services for individuals with disabilities.

Table of Contents

Tables

Figures

Tools

SECTION 1
Foundations

CHAPTER 1
Introduction

The purpose of this book is to familiarize readers with common issues that arise when attempting to grade the performance of students with disabilities, particularly those who are "included" and receive instruction in the regular education classroom, and present strategies for increasing the accuracy, fairness, and meaningfulness of their grades. A majority of the book is dedicated to selecting and implementing "grading adaptations" that can be used for an entire class or for individual students. Finally, the relationship between philosophical and ethical issues related to grading and specific grading procedures is highlighted.

It is the hope that classroom teachers, administrators, and parents can take something from the book that will enhance their insight into the complexities of designing and implementing grading systems for students who often challenge them to be more creative and flexible. The perspectives of regular educators, special educators, administrators, parents, and students on grading practices vary, and throughout this book we attempt to acknowledge the concerns of the entire "team."

Perspective of the Administrator

- Administrators for both general and special education are often responsible for developing and implementing school policies, including those that deal with grading practices. Most schools have some form of a "grading policy," but the scope and detail of such policies vary widely. We will provide specific recommendations for grading policies later, but emphasize here that administrators will find the contents of this book helpful in developing a comprehensive policy.

- Administrators provide both supervision and support to classroom teachers. Support involves problem-solving, often with parents and students, regarding areas of conflict, including grades and grading practices. Administrators will find the concepts and strategies presented here helpful for solving grading-related conflict.

- Administrators may perceive all or part of the information in this book suitable for a professional development event for teachers, such as a workshop or after-school presentation. The author has attempted to make the information accessible and clear for a broad audience, but the opportunity for teachers to discuss and "work through" the many concepts and strategies as a group is highly recommended.

- Administrators must often respond to concerns such as purported grade inflation that arise in the media and professional literature and eventually become the concern of the local community. Those who have knowledge and insight into factors that make grades accurate and meaningful will be better prepared to address political issues regarding grades and grading practices.

Perspective of the General Educator

- General educators seek balance between a well-defined grading sys-

tem that can be communicated clearly to students and parents and the ability to be flexible and use sound judgment when assigning grades on a daily basis. Later we will share research findings indicating that general education teachers do make informal grading adaptations often and in response to the needs of their students. The information presented in this book will help teachers better articulate how and why they are making judgments when grading as they discuss grading with students, parents, and colleagues.

- Diversity in general education classrooms is on the rise, due in part to policies and practices that require students with disabilities to be educated in the general education classroom with maximum access to the general education curriculum. Consequently, general educators face an ongoing need for strategies that help their most challenged students achieve success. This book addresses one of the most visible and controversial symbols of student success – grades – and will help general educators address the diversity of their students.

- The standards-based reform movement currently sweeping our country involves increased emphasis on higher content standards and increased accountability for both students and teachers. In such a climate, administrators and teachers often feel increased responsibility to use accommodations or supports that directly influence student performance on learning standards or large-scale assessments. Ways to link grading adaptations to learning standards are described in this book, as are other strategies for increasing student accountability while also making grades more meaningful.

Perspective of the Special Educator

- Special educators often find themselves in the role of teacher and advocate for their students, particularly in the complex and more competitive culture of general education. For special educators, issues related to the accuracy and fairness of grades are ever-present, as they are the first to hear complaints from students and parents about low grades. This book attempts to describe a variety of grading adaptations that can be implemented collaboratively by the general and special educators, thereby absolving the special educator of total responsibility for making grades fair and meaningful for students with disabilities.

- Special educators may feel obligated to help students with disabilities get passing or high grades, but at the same time be hesitant to use special grading adaptations that allow the student to get a higher grade without showing any change in motivation or performance. This dilemma may be avoided by using one or more of the grading adaptations described in this book that link grading to very specific changes in the student's performance. By following the evaluation tool presented here, special educators can comfortably recommend a grading adaptation that requires a commitment on the part of the student and parent to improve or maintain performance in the classroom.

Perspective of the Parent

- Although parents are not the primary target readership for this book, many may use its contents to effectively advocate for their child. For most parents, grading practices or systems seem both complex and precise, and many would be surprised to know that teacher judgment plays an important role in grading students, particularly those of diverse abilities. Parents often approach grading issues informed only by their own experiences as school-aged students. As a result, when parents' abilities and achievements are very different than those of their child with disabilities, a fresh perspective on the purposes for grades and the impact of grading adaptations may be needed.

Most importantly, parents should find the suggested strategies to be logical and practical, and free of complex jargon or procedures that limit their ability to discuss grading adaptations with their child's teachers.

How to Use This Book

Readers considering this book will likely ask, "Do I have to read the whole book to make sense out of what it says?" The answer is no. However, in deciding what to read, consider how much you already know about grading issues and grading adaptations. To help you in this effort, Figure 1 presents a visual organizer of the book, whereas Figure 2 presents a guide that allows you to select the chapters that are most relevant to your interests or needs at the moment. By reviewing these organizers, you will be able to choose a place to begin reading.

Chapters 2 and 3 are intended to provoke thinking about grading practices and to help sensitize the reader to the perspectives of the other stakeholders in a grading system. For example, educators or parents who are interested in advocating for changes in the way that students with disabilities are graded might find the information in these chapters helpful for building an argument or rationale to present to school administrators or other educators.

Chapters 4 and 5 provide detailed information on types of grading adaptations, the featured interventions in this book. These chapters create a context for the nuts-and-bolts information in Chapters 6 - 10, and are therefore critical to understanding the rest of the book. Don't skip these chapters!

Chapters 6 - 10 present detailed procedures for developing and implementing specific types of grading adaptations. Readers who understand the important features of each type of grading adaptation might choose to focus only on adaptations they perceive to be helpful for their students. In this sense, Chapters 6 - 10 represents a cookbook that contains five recipes from which readers can choose.

Chapter 11 includes information on a variety of topics related to calculating and reporting grades and the use of rubrics. Because of the summative nature of this chapter, it is most useful to readers who are familiar with information presented earlier, particularly in Chapters 1 - 4.

Figure 1
Overview of the Text

Task	Chapter	Outcome
Identifying real issues reported by teachers, students and parents.	Chapter 2	Discussion of types of grading issues.
Clarifying your philosophical beliefs about the purpose or meaning of symbol grades.	Chapter 3	Perceptions of what grades can, should, and do communicate.
Familiarzing yourself with different types of grading adaptation and the benefits and limitations of each.	Chapter 4	Description of types of grading adaptations.
Using a checklist of potential benefits to rate each type of adaption and choose one or more that meets the needs of your students, teachers, and parents.	Chapter 5	Evaluating grading adaptations.
Implementing a specific type of grading adaptation.	Chapter 6	Prioritizing content and related assignments.
	Chapter 7	Balancing product, process, and effort.
	Chapter 8	Measuring and grading progress on IEP objectives.
	Chapter 9	Measuring and grading improvement.
	Chapter 10	Changing scales and weights.
Summarizing and reporting student grades.	Chapter 11	Issues in calculating and reporting grades.
Developing personalized grading plans.	Chapter 12	The PGP model for collaborative development of personalized grading plans.
Clarifying grading issues and making an action plan.	Chapter 13	Applying the principles in this book to grading stories in the news.

Figure 2
A Guide for Using the Book

If you are asking yourself...	... then you will find this chapter helpful
"Why would a general educator or administrator need to know about grading adaptations?"	• Chapters 1 and 2 provide a rationale for and overview of grading adaptations. • Chapter 11 discusses current issues in reporting grades.
"Aren't grading adaptations just another way to 'water down' the general education curriculum so students with disabilities can get higher grades?"	• Chapters 4 and 5 describe how grading adaptations can improve student learning on the general education curriculum. • Chapters 6 and 7 describe how adaptations can focus attention on content-specific learning.
"Shouldn't grades be based only on how much the student has learned?"	• Chapter 3 describes how grades can serve many different purposes. • Chapter 5 describes how to evaluate the helpfulness of adaptations and how to address issues of fairness.
"Should teachers ever use their judgment when grading students?"	• Chapters 1 and 2 describe how systematic use of judgment is instrumental in an effective grading system for all students.
"Can a grading system be updated to include how a student uses technology?"	• Chapter 7 describes how a student's use of assistive technology can be incorporated into your grading system.
"Is there a 'right' way and 'wrong' way to make a grading adaptation?"	• Chapters 6 - 10, 12 provide "field-tested" tools designed to guide you in designing and implementing grading adaptations.
"Won't students with disabilities use grading adaptations as a 'crutch'?"	• Concerns about how grading adaptations can facilitate or impede independence are discussed in Chapter 5. • Chapters 8 - 10 describe special concerns regarding adaptations involving effort, improvement, and a modified grading scale.

Chapter 12 is dedicated to a model for grading students with disabilities. The Personalized Grading Plan (PGP) process facilitates the development of personalized grading plans that include specific grading adaptations. In addition, specific responsibilities are described for each team member to enhance implementation and monitoring of the plan. This innovative model incorporates all strategies in previous chapters into a coherent and streamlined series of activities.

In recognition of the challenging nature of many grading issues, Chapter 13 is devoted to the application of the principles in this book to recent news accounts where concerns about grading practices and policies have appeared in local newspapers. These real-life stories offer a fitting conclusion as readers finish this book and seek to apply the concepts in their own schools.

Each chapter concludes with a list of "Suggested Activities" designed to help readers become more familiar with the concepts and strategies described in the chapter. In many cases, the activities have been suggested by participants in our research projects, or are part of the workshops we have developed for the projects.

The Appendices at the end of the book contain a number of reproduc-ible tools and forms to help readers apply the strategies and other information gleaned from this book to their own situations.

Terms Used in the Book

Several terms are repeated throughout the book and warrant clarification before we get started. The terms were chosen carefully to reflect current usage in the educational literature and not to add validity or credibility to any term. Following are important terms and what they mean in this book.

- *Student with a disability* refers to any student with a disability that qualifies the student for special education services. The strategies presented in this book are most relevant to students with mild-moderate disabilities, but the underlying principles may be relevant for grading students with severe-multiple disabilities.

- *Included student with a disability* refers to any student with a disability who is educated in the general education classroom for at least part of the day (elementary level) or in general education classes for some content areas (middle and secondary level). Although the term "included" is sometimes used to indicate a certain amount of time in the regular education classroom, its use here is not so restrictive.

- *Grading system* refers to the collection of procedures that are used in a school to assign and report grades. The system includes the grading policy and guidelines for the entire school, the specific guidelines and procedures used by classroom teachers, and any specific procedures that are used for individual students. Thus, a grading system is schoolwide. Use of an electronic grading system or the format for progress monitoring forms or report cards are parts of the grading system for the school.

- *Grading practices* refers to the procedures that an individual educator uses in the classroom. Thus, grading practices will vary from class to class. Grading practices include deciding what student performances will be evaluated for a grade, how performance will be translated into a grade, and how much flexibility and judgment will be used when grading. Grading practices are part of the schoolwide grading system.

The Relationship Between Grading Policies, Systems and Practices

Any educational intervention is more likely to be used consistently if it is supported by school policy and is considered a feature of the school's "culture." Most schools have a written grading policy that provides guidelines for giving and interpreting grades. Our experience suggests that many grading policies tend to focus on the grading scale and the schedule for reporting grades to parents. Seldom do policies contain specific language regarding use of judgment or a specific adaptation for grading students with disabilities. Thus, even policies that do indicate that teachers or administrators can adapt the way that students with disabilities are graded are not effective, due to lack of specificity about types of adaptations and when they are appropriate.

In addition to the typical description of the scale and schedule for reporting, a useful grading policy should possess the following features:

- A statement indicating the purpose for grades and how students and parents should interpret them;

- A description of acceptable grading practices, including grading adaptations; and

- Clear guidelines for implementing grading adaptations.

We agree with the recommendation of Salend and Duhaney (2002) that committees composed of educators, students, parents, and community members develop a grading policy by first establishing what everyone wants grades to mean for a given school and community. A grading policy committee must be diverse if it is to represent different perspectives on the fairness of grading practices, particularly adaptations.

Legal Guidelines for Grading

Legal guidelines for grading practices are described in Section 504, in Title II of the Americans with Disabilities Act, and have been summarized by Salend and Duhaney (2002). Individualizing the grading system for students with disabilities is permitted if documented in the student's IEP, thereby representing approval by the team of student, parents and teachers. Practitioners should avoid grading adaptations not approved by the IEP team. Guidelines for grading practices for students without IEPs indicate that grading modifications can be used if made available to all students, and not just individual students (Salend & Duhaney, 2002). Use of any grading modifications should occur only with the approval of school administrators.

Where Do We Go From Here?

The next chapter will describe the prevalent issues related to grading all students, and particularly those with disabilities.

CHAPTER 2
Overview of Grading Issues

Perhaps no topic related to educational practice generates as much discussion or debate as grading. One obvious reason for the prevalence of opinions regarding grading is that we all have expertise in the area–we have all received grades. Some of us also are or have been parents of children who received grades, providing us with even more self-proclaimed knowledge and expertise on the topic. So given the fact that all or most individuals have experience with, and hold an opinion regarding, grading practices and grades, it seems logical to expect that a significant body of research on grading practices would have been compiled in the past century. Thus, we might expect that "best practices" for grading would be available, informing consistent grading practices. However, debate regarding "best practices" for grading continues even though an extensive body of literature does exist (e.g., Azwell & Schmar, 1995; Carpenter, 1985; Gersten, Vaughn, & Brengelman, 1996; Guskey & Bailey, 2001; Marzano, 2000). Thus, in approaching the topic of grading practices for students with disabilities, we acknowledge that numerous grading issues exist for all students, parents, and teachers, and that no simple solution is likely to be identified.

Grading Issues: Something for Everyone

In their comprehensive text on grading and reporting systems, Guskey and Bailey (2001) describe the following chronic issues with grading systems for general education classrooms: (a) teachers receive minimal preparation in their preservice programs on how to develop grading systems; hence they rely on their personal philosophies and experiences when grading their students; (b) teachers often perceive grading to be time-consuming, and in conflict with their primary responsibilities as teachers; and (c) parents report that they want more frequent and detailed feedback than is typically provided.

Marzano (2000) cites the following pervasive problems with grading systems in general education classes: (a) teachers include factors other than academic achievement (e.g., effort, behavior) in an inconsistent fashion when grading; (b) teachers assign different values or weights to similar assignments so that students with similar performances in different classes may receive different grades; and (c) teachers place too much emphasis on a single score to reflect student performance.

Additional common issues are that (a) students and parents are often unaware of the grading system being used in their child's classroom; and (b) teachers often deviate, sometimes for good reason, from the grading system described for the class (Friedman & Truog, 1999). Clearly, significant issues with grading persist despite decades of research and the collective wisdom of experienced teachers and administrators.

Unfortunately, issues related to grading of students with disabilities (e.g., learning disabilities, emotional or behavioral disabilities, mild cognitive disabilities), particularly those who are included in a general education class, extend beyond those for all students, and reflect the complexity of meeting the needs of these students in a general education setting. In the following section we will review some common issues.

Grading Issues for Included Students with Disabilities: Fuel on the Fire!

Grading issues for "included" students with disabilities are particularly complex because they include those described above for all students, as well as numerous others unique to grading students with disabilities. Research has described the following issues related to grading students with disabilities:

• Included students often receive low or failing grades.

Many included students, particularly at the secondary level, receive low or failing grades in their general education classes. Chronic low grades can negatively impact a student's motivation to try hard, and as a result, may lead to debate among team members regarding the appropriateness of inclusion in the general education classroom (Donahue & Zigmond, 1990). The issue of low grades has come to the forefront recently with the nationwide debate on "social promotion," in which students are passed on to the next grade regardless of failing grades. As policies eliminating this practice are implemented, teachers are struggling to find ways to support students with disabilities in obtaining passing grades.

- Grades serve different purposes for the student, parents, or teachers.

Students, parents, and teachers often expect grades to provide different types of information. For example, a student may expect a grade to reflect how hard they tried in class, while his father may expect his son's grade to reflect how much of the general education curriculum his son completed during a given marking period (Calhoun, 1986; Frisbie & Waltman, 1992; Hendrickson & Gable, 1997; Marzano, 2000; Munk & Bursuck, 1998a, 1998b, 2001b; Rojewski, Pollard, & Meers, 1992; Salend & Duhaney, 2002). The many purposes for grades are also a problem because they lead to confusion and dissatisfaction with the grading system and become a source of conflict between the student, parents, and teachers. Although grades have and will hold different meanings to different individuals, this potential issue can be addressed through improved communication regarding the grading system.

- Teachers feel pressure to give passing or inflated grades to students with disabilities because the work is difficult in general education classes.

The author's experiences suggest that teachers in inclusive classrooms may follow an unwritten philosophy that students with disabilities should receive at least a passing grade. The source of this philosophy seems to be the teachers' perceptions that students who are placed in the challenging situation of the general classroom deserve a "safety net" in the event that the work is too difficult (Calhoun, 1986; Munk & Bursuck, 2001a). The practice of assuring a passing grade, no matter what, is a problem because it prevents schools from focusing on the real issue that students with disabilities are performing poorly in the general education classroom. We have encountered teachers who have made a convincing argument that giving a student with a disability a failing grade does not result in any change in instruction or services, and may actually cause the student to stop working hard or even leave school. Thus, there are different perspectives on guaranteeing passing grades to included students with disabilities; however, we can all agree that the student is best served by interventions that result in "legitimate" passing grades.

- The system or processes used to grade included students may not be linked to their curricular or instructional modifications.

Individualized Education Programs (IEPs) for included students typically contain a description of the supports to be provided in the general education classroom. Examples of common supports include extra time to complete work, presentation of information in written and oral modalities, individual instruction on strategies, or modified assignments. Often, the products of the student's work, regardless of the amount or type of support that is provided, are graded using the same criteria as those for the rest of the class. While this may be appropriate when the student is completing the same assignment as the rest of the class, but with supports (e.g., having a test read aloud), using the same grading process may be less appropriate when the student is expected to follow a different path to completing an assignment. For example, Jill has an IEP objective involving use of a strategy for editing her work before turning it in for grading. If she receives a grade only on the final paper she turns in, that grade may not reflect her actual proficiency with the strategy. If the grading process for Jill were linked to her IEP, she might receive two grades for her writing assignment: one grade for the quality of the final product and another for her proficiency with the editing strategy (Bradley & Calvin, 1998; Munk & Bursuck, 2001a). This issue may reflect a general failure to integrate the IEP into the general education classroom.

• The grading process for included students may not consider progress on the learning objectives on the IEP.

The author's experiences suggest that the notion of basing a student's grades on progress on learning objectives in the IEP may cause debate among team members. Underlying the debate are differing perceptions of the validity of IEP objectives to drive instruction and reflect actual student needs. For example, Jill, a sixth grader, has an objective for "solving multistep math problems involving addition, subtraction, multiplication, or division." Criteria for meeting the objective are "90% accuracy for 10 consecutive opportunities." If her team wants to base all or part of her math grade on her progress on this objective, they must schedule opportunities for Jill to work on such problems and regular assessments must be given (Bradley & Calvin, 1998; Munk, Bursuck, & Silva, 2003; Salend & Duhaney, 2002). Our own research has underlined general educators' lack of knowledge of content of the IEPs of students in their classes (Munk, et al., 2003).

• General and special educators may not collaborate or communicate in determining how a student with a disability could or should be graded.

General and special educators often experience role confusion when it comes to grading students in regular classes. Special educators may defer to the general educator because it is "their class." General educators may lack knowledge of options for grading adaptations, but may not seek help from their colleagues. One scenario we have encountered has the special education teacher submitting a separate grade for work during a "resource" period that is then added to the grade for work in the regular classroom. In this scenario, minimal communication is occurring (Christiansen & Vogel, 1988; Drucker & Hansen, 1982; Munk & Bursuck, 2001a). Although ongoing collaboration is not a necessity for improving the grading system for an inclusive classroom, some communication regarding the strengths and limitations of students with disabilities is necessary for the general educator to be able to design an effective grading system that accommodates those students.

• Students and parents may have no input into how the student will be graded.

When a student and the student's parents are satisfied with grades assigned by the teacher, they may be unlikely to suggest changes in the grading process. Traditionally, grading has been viewed as the privilege of the classroom teacher, who possesses the professional judgment necessary to assign grades (Bietau, 1995). Conversely, teachers often view students and parents as lacking knowledge and objectivity when discussing grading. Given their historical alienation from the grading system for themselves and their children, parents' negative perceptions of report card grades are not surprising (Munk & Bursuck, 2001b). However, research has found that in fact, students and parents can participate in decision-making about grading processes (Munk & Bursuck, 2001a).

In summary, the scope of issues related to grading included students is broad, including not only the procedures that are used to determine grades, but also the interpretation of the grades themselves. Thus, a model for intervening on grading issues must allow for flexibility and team decision-making, rather than a formula for grading all students in the same manner. It is just such a model that we have investigated in our research (Munk & Bursuck, 2001a; Munk, et al., 2003) and will describe in this book.

A Proposed Solution to Grading Issues for Included Students

The term "effective" will be used to describe a grading system that includes steps and procedures to avoid or minimize the many issues we have discussed.

The following are important characteristics of an effective grading system for included students:

- The system is designed to focus on what is most important for the student to do and learn. That is, the system promotes *accountability* for students, parents, and teachers.

- The system produces grades that are perceived by the student, parents, and teacher to be an *accurate and fair* representation of the student's performance in the classroom.

- The system includes a *mechanism for exchanging information* between the student, parents, and teachers.

- The system includes *guidelines for implementing* an array of grading practices and alternatives.

- The system *clarifies the purpose for grades and the potential effects* that grades will have on a student's motivation, self-esteem, and future performance. Hence, grades are *meaningful and fair.*

We propose that a comprehensive approach to designing an effective grading system for included students will consist of (a) grading adaptations that are selected or designed to address a student's particular needs, (b) a plan for systematically monitoring and communicating student progress, and (c) a process that involves the student, parents, and teachers in a collaborative effort to implement components (a) and (b). In our research on personalized grading plans (Munk & Bursuck, 2001a; Munk et al., 2003), we have observed the potential for grading adaptations to improve the level and accuracy of a student's grade. In addition, we have observed the potential for students and parents to collaborate with the general and special educators to identify how students' strengths and limitations interact with the demands (e.g., taking tests, completing projects, note-taking) of a particular class to produce individual assignment and report card grades that are more or less accurate, fair, satisfactory, or motivating.

Individualizing or personalizing a grading system is central to our approach to grading students with disabilities. Researchers (e.g., Marzano, 2000) have argued against including factors other than content-specific learning when grading students in general education. A student's performance on the classroom curriculum should always be the primary determinant for a grade. However, grading adaptations can also be used to enhance content-specific learning by a student with a disability, sometimes by including non-achievement factors such as effort in the grading system. The compatibility of our model for grading with the "best practices" for grading in general education is explained throughout the book.

The importance of collaboration between the student, parents, and teachers is referred to several times in the book. Potential benefits of collaboration between the general and special educator in selecting or designing a personalized grading plan for an included student will be cited. At the same time, important changes in grading practices can be initiated by a motivated teacher or parent, armed with a clear notion of what is wrong with the current grading system and ideas for how to develop an improved system. Such individuals can initiate discussions or implement changes in how an individual student is graded, and can become a change agent for their colleagues and school. Thus, we encourage readers not to become disheartened if the procedures we describe in this book seem to require significant collaboration–change can begin with just one individual with an idea!

The rest of this book, will "unpack" the process of implementing personalized grading plans by introducing key components in the process, along with a discussion of research findings and philosophical perspectives that help to inform practitioners when revising or developing grading systems. The process starts with a philosophical issue – what grades can or should communicate, then progresses to grading adaptations, the primary "intervention" in the personalized grading system.

Chapter Summary

This chapter described the many issues involved in the grading of all students, and particularly those with disabilities. The scope of issues is broad, and includes both philosophical and practical issues. A model for improving a grading system must be comprehensive and able to address many problems as perceived by the student, parents, and teachers. Reading and understanding the issues presented in this chapter are the first steps in evaluating and improving your own grading system.

Suggested Activities

The following activities will allow you to learn more about grading issues in your school and to pinpoint issues within your own classroom:

- Discuss grading issues with your colleagues. You may bring up the topic at a meeting or exchange ideas electronically with e-mail or a discussion group. Ask them what experiences they have had with students and parents and how they have changed their grading systems over time. You may want to create a brief survey of items that you want each colleague to address.

- Consider whether a review of your school's grading system might be helpful for you and your colleagues. You might raise the question at your department meeting to find out if others are interested in the topic. Chances are, some colleagues will not even be familiar with your school's grading policy.

- Evaluate your school's grading policy for details and guidelines. Look for any language regarding the purpose for grades. Most grading policies lack detail, and improving your policy may seem important to your colleagues.

- Brainstorm ideas for increasing participation by your students and their parents in the grading process for your classroom or school. You might start by identifying how or when they are notified of your grading system. Then consider what types of input they could provide to improve your system.

- Read additional materials regarding grading systems. You will find many sources in the reference list at the end of this book.

Where Do We Go From Here?

The next chapter will take an in-depth look at one of the more prominent issues with grades – grades can serve different purposes and communicate different information to different people. That is, we all make different judgments about what a C means. Consider how your colleagues, students, and parents perceive grades as you design or improve the grading system for your school or classroom.

CHAPTER 3
Perceptions of What Grades Can, Should and Do Communicate

The Case of Maria

Maria is a 7th-grade student with a learning disability who is included in the general science class. Today Maria brought her report on recycling home to show her parents. Maria proudly hands them the report, for which she received 85 of 100 points, or a B+. Maria's mom is very pleased and praises Maria for her hard work on the project. As Maria's dad reads her report, he looks confused. Finally, he says that he has found many spelling and grammatical errors and that he can't believe that Maria's teacher didn't take off more points for the errors. Maria's mom jumps in to defend Maria and explains that because of Maria's difficulties with spelling and writing, her teacher marks errors but does not subtract points, or allows Maria to correct the errors. Maria's father expresses his concern that, "I should be able to look at a grade on a paper and know how well Maria did on the same work as her classmates. Isn't that what grades are for?" Maria's mom, sensing Maria's disappointment with her father's reaction, points out that "grades should be based on how hard a student tries, too." After all, "How fair would it be for Maria to always receive low grades because spelling and writing are so hard for her?"

Purposes of Grades

Another way of saying that grades have different purposes is to say that they may provide different information or meaning to different people. Discussion of the multiple purposes for grades as the source of much confusion and conflict have appeared in the professional literature for decades (e.g., Airasian, 1994; Bradley & Calvin, 1998; Carpenter, 1985; Marzano, 2000; Munk & Bursuck, 2001b; Stiggins, Frisbie, & Griswold, 1989; Terwilliger, 1977). We all interpret grades somewhat differently because we have a different perception of what grades should mean or communicate, and therefore we are confused or frustrated when grades seem to mean something different. When individual team members possess different perceptions of the purpose for grades, as was the case for Maria's parents, it can be more difficult to reach consensus on whether the grading process being used for a student will produce an accurate or fair grade.

Because there is no single best purpose for grades, it is important that team members acknowledge their own perceptions of purposes for grades, and that the team discuss differences in perceptions and attempt to reach an understanding of what grades should mean. The purpose of the following exercise is not necessarily to reach agreement on a single purpose for grades, but to make sure that each team member can clarify his or her own perceptions and compare them to those of others.

Clarifying the Perceived Purposes for Grades

The steps for clarifying the perceived purposes for grades include: (a) taking the survey of purposes for grades, (b) scoring your results, (c) interpreting your results, and (d) comparing results for each team member.

Step 1: Taking the Survey

The parent version of the Survey of Grading Purposes appears in Tool 3-1. (Reproducible tools for parents, teachers, and students appear in Appendix B.) We have included this version to emphasize the importance of finding out how parents perceive grades before beginning discussion of possible adaptations. Please read the instructions carefully when completing the survey (Tool 3-1 Part 1) and read the next section to interpret your responses (Tool 3-1 Part 2).

Step 2: Scoring Your Rankings

Purposes included in the survey may be clustered into three areas: academic performance, affective and behavioral competencies, or directions for transition and post-secondary planning. The second part of Tool 3-1 presents items representing each of the three focus areas. You can score your survey by placing your rank for each purpose in the far right column and then adding the ranks for each focus area. Once you have recorded and summed your rankings, the focus area with the lowest sum of ranks may be interpreted as most important to you. An alternative method involves considering only the top 3-5 rankings and in which focus areas they fall. This method allows you to focus on separate purposes from different areas, rather than on just one area. In reality, grading systems, particularly those that have been individualized to a student's needs, can produce grades that meet purposes from more than one focus area.

Tool 3-1
Survey of Grading Purposes: Parent Version, Part 1

Instructions: Rank the 12 purposes in order of importance by writing a number 1-12 next to each purpose (1= most important, 12 = least important). Use each number only once.

Purposes for Grades   Ranking

1. Tell me whether my child has improved in his/her classes.   Rank___

2. Tell me how to help my child plan for his/her future.   Rank___

3. Tell me how hard my child is trying.   Rank___

4. Tell me what my child needs to improve on to keep a good grade. Rank___

5. Tell me how well my child works with classmates.   Rank___

6. Tell me what my child is good at and not so good at.   Rank___

7. Tell colleges and employers what my child is good at.   Rank___

8. Tell me how much my child can do on his/her own.   Rank___

9. Tell me how my child's performance compares to other children.   Rank___

10. Tell me how much of the general curriculum my child mastered.   Rank___

11. Tell me what classes my child should take in high school.   Rank___

12. Motivate my child to try harder.   Rank___

Tool 3-1
Survey of Grading Purposes: Parent Version, Part 2

Instructions: Transfer your rankings from Part 1 to the interpretive chart in Part 2. Sum the ranks for the items in each Focus Area. The lower the score, the more important that Focus Area is perceived.

Focus Area: Academic Performance

Item	Ranking
1. Tell me whether my child has improved in his/her classes.	_____
9. Tell me how my child's performance compares to other children.	_____
10. Tell me how much of the general curriculum my child mastered.	_____
8. Tell me how much my child can do on his/her own.	_____
Total	_____

Focus Area: Affective and Behavioral

Item	Ranking
5. Tell me how well my child works with classmates.	_____
3. Tell me how hard my child is trying.	_____
12. Motivate my child to try harder.	_____
4. Tell me what my child needs to improve on to keep a good grade.	_____
Total	_____

Focus Area: Transition and Postsecondary Planning

Item	Ranking
2. Tell me how to help my child plan for his/her future.	_____
11. Tell me what classes my child should take in high school.	_____
7. Tell colleges and employers what my child is good at.	_____
6. Tell me what my child is good at and not so good at.	_____
Total	_____

Step 3: Interpreting Your Results

Implications of the three focus areas include:

Academic performance: Purposes in this focus area reflect an interest in monitoring performance on the academic expectations for the class.

Affective and behavioral: Purposes in this focus area reflect an interest in the student's proficiency with important survival skills and the student's effort.

Transition and post-secondary planning: Purposes in this focus area reflect an interest in interpreting and using grades to predict future performance and to identify areas of strength and limitation.

Step 4: Comparing Results for Each Team Member

When several team members complete surveys, results should be discussed. It is important that team members understand each other's rankings. When significant differences exist, team members may wish to give a rationale for their ranking. For example, a parent who ranked purposes in the affective and behavioral area much lower may feel that her son's effort should be rewarded in the grading process. In contrast, a parent who ranks purposes in the area for directing transition and postsecondary planning may be thinking ahead to career planning and college admissions, and looking to grades to inform his child and himself of potential areas of interest and strength. In the next section we will describe research findings on perceived purposes for grades. We can also share several trends we have noted in how students, teachers, and parents perceive purposes for grades and the rationale they give for their perceptions.

When one parent spends more time than his or her spouse helping the student with homework or communicating with the teachers about performance, that parent is more likely to feel that the student's grades should reflect effort and be motivating for the student. This is not surprising given that the more involved parent observes the student struggling with schoolwork and has to provide support for the work to get done. The less involved parent may not be aware of the student's struggle in school, and in many cases is more reluctant to have a grade reflect anything but progress on the general education curriculum. Indeed, most of the negotiating regarding purposes for grades in our projects has occurred between parents, rather teachers.

To date, we have not established any clear pattern in the responses for special educators and general educators. One impression that has emerged is that teachers seem to hold a "global" view of purposes for report card grades that applies to all students. Special or general educators who feel that a grade should serve a particular purpose (e.g., communicate effort) tend to adhere to that perception for all students and to pursue grading adaptations that are consistent with their perception.

What Role does Purpose Play in Grading Students with Disabilities?

It is difficult to gauge how much emphasis to place on perceived purposes for grades when developing grading systems. One perspective is that communities should have a voice in determining what purpose grades should serve and in subsequently developing the actual grading systems for local schools (Guskey & Bailey, 2001; Salend & Duhaney, 2002). In such a scenario, parents and students would strive for consensus on whether, for example, grades should reflect each student's performance on the same assignments and therefore could be used to "compare" students in the same class. If the consensus favored a grading system that was based on progress on individual goals, and not necessarily common assignments, teams would have to develop individualized grading systems for each student.

While the latter scenario seems ideal, it is not feasible given the many responsibilities already placed on teachers. And even if a group can reach consensus on a grading policy and system, some members will continue to have differing opinions, especially if the grading system is not perceived as "working" for their child. We investigated the potential effects of their child's school achievement on parents' perceptions of report card grades (Munk & Bursuck, 2002) by surveying parents of high achieving (GPA 4.0 - 3.25), average achieving (GPA 3.24 - 2.5) and low achieving (GPA below 2.5) students without disabilities and a group of parents of students with disabilities. Specifically, we asked parents to rank by importance 10 purposes for report card grades (we have since expanded the survey to include 12 items), and to indicate on a 6-point scale (1 = very ineffective, 6 = very effective) how effectively their children's grades met each purpose. Table 1 presents our findings for the combined achievement groups of students without disabilities and those with disabilities.

Regarding the importance of the purposes, parents of students without disabilities ranked Purpose 9 (convey your child's abilities to postsecondary schools or employers) significantly higher than did their counterparts. Although differences were not statistically significant for

Table 1
Parent Perceptions of Purposes for Report Card Grades

Purposes for report card grades	Mean rankings of importance			Mean rankings of effectiveness		
	Without disability	With disability	p	Without disability	With disability	p
1. Communicate general achievement and quality of work on the high school curriculum	3.76	4.00	.64	4.44	3.63	.00
2. Communicate your child's efforts and work habits	3.29	2.94	.36	4.46	4.00	.08
3. Motivate your child to keep working	5.26	4.91	.49	3.84	3.63	.50
4. Communicate progress on individual goals or mastery of specific content	3.78	4.15	.40	3.84	3.22	.06
5. Communicate how your child's performance compares to that of other students	7.24	7.94	.17	2.75	2.56	.55
6. Communicate your child's strengths/needs and provide feedback on how to improve	3.47	2.76	.04	3.13	3.50	.27
7. Provide direction for planning for your child's after-school life	8.14	7.36	.07	2.64	2.25	.22
8. Provide information to teachers for planning instruction	6.79	6.88	.83	2.87	2.94	.82
9. Convey your child's abilities to postsecondary schools or employers	6.90	8.24	.00	3.63	2.38	.00
10. Provide information to teachers about which students may need special help or programs	6.18	5.36	.09	3.78	3.66	.67

Source: Munk, D. & Bursuck, W.D. (2001). What report card grades should and do communicate: Perceptions of parents of secondary students with and without disabilities. *Remedial and Special Education, 22*, 280-286. Reprinted with permission of Pro-Ed, Inc.

Purpose 6, the mean rankings do suggest that parents of students with disabilities thought report card grades should communicate their child's strengths/needs and provide feedback. Regarding effectiveness, parents of students without disabilities questioned whether grades communicate general achievement and quality work on the high school curriculum (Purpose 1), or are effective for conveying their child's abilities to postsecondary schools or employers (Purpose 9).

In looking at whether achievement level affected perceptions, we found that parents of high-achieving students ascribed more importance to Purpose 10, and thought that grades met that purpose. It is interesting that parents of both high and low achieving students thought grades are effective at communicating their children's effort and work habits (Purpose 2). The considerable agreement between groups of parents in the study seems to support the notion that the issue of multiple meanings for grades is common to students in both general and special education, and that, in general, parents are somewhat skeptical of the effectiveness of grades for meeting any of the defined purposes.

Based on our research and the recommendations that appear in the professional literature, we offer the suggestions presented in Table 2 for incorporating this topic into the development, clarification, or individualization of your grading system.

Chapter Summary

This chapter described the various meanings for grades and presented a tool for surveying colleagues, students, and parents about what grades mean to them. This information is presented early on in the book because clarifying what team members expect a grade to tell them will help in selecting an appropriate and meaningful grading adaptation.

Suggested Activities

The following activities are suggested for learning more about purposes for grades or for getting started on making changes to your current grading system:

• Introduce Tool 3-1 at a team or department meeting and discuss your colleagues' rankings. Realizing that teachers in the same school, or even the same classroom, hold differing opinions about the purposes for grades may be a starting point for further discussion of the school grading policy.

• Ask your students what they think their grades mean. Look for evidence that achievement level or school experiences influence a student's perceptions of grades.

Table 2
How and When to Consider Multiple Purposes for Grades

Clarifying perceived purposes for grades, particularly report card grades, can be helpful in several different ways and can be pursued for different reasons. In general, clarification serves to promote consistent grading practices among teachers, and to help parents interpret their children's grades accurately. Both of these uses may also prevent misinterpretation, dissatisfaction, or distrust between the student, parents, and school.

Here are ways and reasons to pursue clarification on the meaning of grades in your school:

Survey and discuss among teachers and administrators when your school is developing or elaborating its grading policies.
- Use discussion to inform the wording of your grading policy. Consider soliciting perceptions from teachers, students, parents, and other community members. A committee may be appointed to conduct these activities.
- Use purposes as one criterion for evaluating your policies or systems. Conduct a review of the grades earned by students in your school. Consider whether the grades provide consistent information to parents, and whether any inconsistencies are actually useful and fair.

Survey and discuss among supporting teams of special and general educators who work collaboratively in inclusive classroom.
- Use discussion as part of collaborative decision-making regarding grading the whole class or individual students. Planning instruction for included students should also include planning for grading.
- Use discussion to establish parameters for grading adaptations for students with disabilities. Having teachers share their grading practices can lead to consensus-building on what purposes grades should serve, and how those purposes should be communicated to students and parents.

Survey and discuss among student, parents, and teachers when the team is problem-solving how to improve satisfaction with students' grades.
- Use discussion to identify the causes of dissatisfaction or confusion with the student's grades. Consider having the student and parents complete the grading purpose survey when dissatisfaction with a grade is voiced. Clarifying what everyone wants from grades first can lead to a more productive discussion of how to support the student in the classroom.
- Use discussion to guide the team in selecting grading adaptations for a student. Clarifying what everyone wants grades to communicate is a necessary step to selecting grading adaptations.

- Consider whether your school's grading policy is due for revision and, if so, whether a committee that includes students and parents, as well as teachers, may be appointed. By forming a diverse committee, you are more likely to develop a policy that is based on what the community wants grades to communicate.

Where Do We Go From Here?

Chapters 2 and 3 have described a number of philosophical and practical issues related to grading included students with disabilities. In essence, these chapters have described the breadth of issues surrounding grading, especially philosophical issues that are often ignored when new classroom practices are adopted. The next chapter moves on to describe several types of grading adaptations, each with its own strengths and limitations.

SECTION 2
Developing Grading Adaptations

CHAPTER 4
Grading Adaptations

The term "grading adaptation" has been used to describe a variety of strategies used to assess a student's performance in the classroom and assign grades. Grading adaptations can be made for individual assignments or for determining report card grades. In a sense, the term "adaptation" may be misleading in that it suggests procedures that are different from those used for other students. In reality, grading adaptations are practical and logical strategies that many teachers implement informally as they exercise their professional judgment in assessing and grading students. Research suggests that as many as 50% of general education teachers implement grading adaptations informally, as they see fit (Polloway et al., 1996).

In selecting the specific grading adaptations to include in this book, the following questions were considered: (a) Has research supported the effectiveness or perceived value of the grading adaptation? (b) Does the adaptation have potential to meet all or most of the criteria described in Chapter 3 for an effective grading system? and (c) Does the adaptation have a significant downside or limitation that might negatively impact the student in the future? Adherence to these criteria led to a list of grading adaptations that are slightly modified from those described in other sources (e.g., Friend & Bursuck, 2002; Munk & Bursuck, 1998a, 1998b). Those descriptions of grading adaptations included grading procedures such as portfolio assessment that are not within the scope and focus of this book.

Types of Grading Adaptations

Table 3 displays each of five categories of grading adaptations discussed in detail in subsequent chapters. Adaptations have been grouped into five categories to emphasize the processes and procedures that underlie the adaptations in each cat-

Table 3
Types of Grading Adaptations

Grading adaptations that involve prioritization of content and related assignments (Drucker & Hansen, 1982; Guskey & Bailey, 2001; Munk, Bursuck, & Silva, 2003; Zobroski, 1981)

Adaptations	*Description and Example*
Report Cards Base all or most of the grade on how well the student performed on prioritized content and related assignments.	If you believe that the three experiments in your science class will cover the most important content, the student will spend more time and receive more support on these assignments and they will count more toward the grade.

Grading adaptations that involve components of a balanced grading system (Carpenter, 1985; Frierson, 1975; Gersten, Vaughn, & Brengelman, 1996; Guskey & Bailey, 2001; Hendrickson & Gable, 1997; Horowitz, 1982; Lindsey, Burns, & Guthrie, 1984; Munk & Bursuck, 2001a; Munk, Bursuck, & Silva, 2003; Friedman & Truog, 1999)

Adaptations	*Description and Example*
Daily Work Base all or part of the grade for an assignment on processes used by the student to complete the work.	Base part of the grade for an essay on how well the student completed the planning organizer and edited the first draft.
Base all or part of the grade for an assignment on the student's performance with supports that "build new skills."	Base part of a grade for a research paper on how proficiently the student used the editing functions in the word processing program. For example, assign 15 of the 100 points for the assignment to effective use of spell and grammar checking, thesaurus, or tools for making tasks or graphics.
Base part of the grade for an assignment on the student's effort.	Base part of the grade for a homework assignment in math on the number of word problems attempted. For example, assign 10 of the 100 points for the word problem worksheet to the number of problems completed, with a criteria of 10 problems completed to earn 10 points.

Table 3 (continued)

Grading adaptations that involve progress on IEP objectives (Cohen, 1983; Frierson, 1975; Munk, Bursuck, & Silva, 2003)

Adaptations	*Description and Example*
Daily Work Base all or part of the grade on criteria established for an IEP objective.	Assign an A for a worksheet if the student meets the 85% criterion for using a strategy to correctly solve math problems, as written in his IEP. For example, if the student uses the strategy to complete 17 of 20 problems (85%), she earns an A on the assignment.
Report Card Base all or part of the grade on progress on IEP objectives.	20% of the student's grade in social studies will be determined by progress on the following objective: "Tom will improve his reading comprehension by summarizing and retelling what he has read after each paragraph or section of his textbook." Each time the teachers ask Tom to summarize and retell, they assign a score of 1-3 based on his accuracy. Then these points are added up to compute 20% of his report card grade.

Grading adaptations that involve measuring improvement (Bradley & Calvin, 1998; Frierson, 1975; Lieberman, 1982; Munk & Bursuck, 2001a; Munk, Bursuck, & Silva, 2003; Slavin, 1980)

Adaptations	*Description and Example*
Daily Work Base all or part of the grade on improvement from past assignments.	Make an agreement that if Willard can raise his average quiz score from 60% to 75%, you will add 5% that may allow him to earn a B.
Assign bonus points for meeting or exceeding specified criteria.	Give 5 bonus points for each correct paragraph the student writes beyond the three paragraphs required as part of the student's modified assignment. For example, if the student earned 75 points on the assignment but wrote a 4th paragraph, you add 5 points to raise the score to 80 points.

Table 3 (continued)

Grading adaptations that involve changing scales or weights (Drucker & Hansen, 1982; Munk & Bursuck, 2001a; Munk, Bursuck, & Silva, 2003)

Adaptations	*Description and Example*
Daily Work Change the number of points or percentages required to earn a specified letter grade on an assignment.	Change the grading scale so that a student must earn 90 out of 100 points (90%), rather than 93 points (93%) indicated in the schoolwide grading policy to earn an A.
Report Card Grade Change the number of points or the percentages required to earn a specified report card grade.	Change the grading scale so that a student earning 60% of total points will earn a D rather than an F as indicated in the schoolwide grading policy.
Change the weights assigned to different performance areas.	Change the weights assigned to tests and homework to reduce the penalty to a student who struggles with tests but benefits from doing homework. For example, reduce the weight of tests from 60% to 40% of the grade, and increase homework from 10% to 30%.

egory. Although some overlap in purpose and procedures may exist between adaptations, we believe that placement into categories will help readers understand the thrust of each type of adaptation. Following are descriptions of each type of adaptation, as well as support found in the professional literature.

Grading adaptations that involve prioritization of content and related assignments.

The purpose of adaptations in this category is to focus the grading system for a whole class, group of students, or individual student on specific content and related assignments that have been deemed "most important," or a top priority. The strategy of focusing the grading of students with disabilities on prioritized content has been recommended for two decades in the professional literature (Drucker & Hansen, 1982; Zobroski, 1981), but has not evolved into a common grading practice. Benefits of prioritizing the curriculum prior to grading include the emphasis that can be placed on mastery learning of important content (Drucker & Hansen, 1982) and the increased clarity of grades based on predetermined criteria. Of the grading adaptations described in this book, those that involve prioritization are best suited for emphasizing content-specific learning (Marzano, 2000).

Although the link between deciding what content and related assignments are most important for students to complete and designing the system used to grade student performance may not seem obvious at first glance, the two processes are both interdependent and intertwined. Teachers, parents, and students may not explicitly state their assumption that grades are assigned only to important work, but they are likely making such an assumption. In fact, questions regarding the importance of certain content or assignments may arise only after a student or parent questions how or why a low, inaccurate, or unfair grade was given. To prevent such conflict, or to prepare for effective communication with the student and parents when conflict arises, general educators should be able to (a) state the relative importance of the content they will cover during a specific period (e.g., marking period), and (b) describe the guidelines, rules, or standards used to prioritize the content.

We acknowledge that some teachers may interpret emphasis on prioritization to suggest that a portion of what is taught and assessed in classrooms is "not important." In truth, a focus on prioritization of the classroom content as a first step in developing an effective grading system is an acknowledgment of the varied and complex influences placed on general education teachers to educate a diverse group of learners. For example, decisions regarding what to teach, and then how to prioritize the selected content, are influenced by the presence of state or national learning standards, a district or school curriculum, the scope and sequence of materials used for the class, and the training and interests of the individual teacher (King-Sears, 2001). Further, the extent to which a teacher may "choose" from the above influences may be affected by administrative priorities and varies considerably across schools; thus, the benefit of moving through a process for prioritizing content and related assignments is obvious.

As stated previously, support for prioritizing content when developing an effective grading system for included students with disabilities can be found in the professional literature for general and special education. For example, Guskey and

Bailey (2001) recommend standards-based grading as an alternative grading system for the general education classroom that involves prioritization of content. These authors describe the following four-step process for implementing standards-based grading:

1. Identify the major learning goals or standards that students will be expected to achieve at each grade level or in each course of study.

2. Establish performance indicators for the learning goals or standards.

3. Determine graduated levels of quality (benchmarks) for assessing each goal or standard.

4. Develop reporting tools that communicate teachers' judgment of students' learning progress and culminating achievement in relation to the learning goals or standards. (p. 84)

The initial step of identifying learning goals and standards represents one method for prioritizing content and related assignments for grading. The authors point out that many school districts now emphasize standards-based instruction and grading. Thus, teachers are expected to prioritize the "universe" of potential content, available in both classroom materials and the teacher's knowledge, based on alignment with the learning standards for the district or school.

Guskey and Bailey (2001) also point out that where multiple sources of learning standards exist, confusion over which to follow may result. In Illinois, for example, the state board of education issues learning standards for each content area, and schools are expected to adopt classroom curriculum materials that prepare students to meet those standards. In areas where individual districts, schools, or even teachers are expected to generate learning standards, diversity in approaches and opinions may be expected. In such situations, clarifying how the teacher has prioritized classroom content may be even more central to developing an effective grading system.

Prioritizing classroom content and related assignments for shorter periods of time, such as units or lessons, has been recommended as an effective practice for serving students with disabilities in general education classrooms (Schumm, Vaughn, & Harris, 1994). The rationale for prioritizing content to be covered in a unit or individual lesson is that students with disabilities often must expend more time and energy to access and understand material than nondisabled peers. Thus, any steps the teacher takes to focus the student on the most important content, and possibly to limit the amount of material to be attempted by the student, should facilitate increased success.

Vaughn and colleagues (1994) have developed the Planning Pyramid to guide teachers in prioritizing what will be taught and what students must do for a unit or lesson. We will describe this tool in Chapter 6, which is dedicated wholly to processes and procedures for prioritization. The relationship between prioritization and grading is straightforward: Content and assignments that are considered most important should also be assessed for the purpose of grading. Furthermore, the extent to which a student's grades reflect progress/mastery on the general education curriculum may be enhanced if based on content that is deemed to be most relevant. At a minimum, prioritizing prior to developing a grading system allows the classroom teacher to say, with confidence, that the students' grades will reflect performance on content that is (a) aligned with specified learning standards, (b) considered important by professional organizations, or (c) considered prerequisite for entry into higher level classes in the district.

Grading adaptations that involve components of a balanced grading system.

Before launching into the specifics of how to "balance" your grading system, a definition for "grading system" is needed. The definition used in this book has been influenced by researchers in both general education (e.g., Guskey & Bailey, 2001) and special education (e.g., Carpenter, 1985; Hendrickson & Gable, 1997; Mehring, 1995), who have suggested that an effective grading system must consider different types of student performances in determining grades for individual assignments (formative assessment) and report card grades (summative assessment). A common structure for an effective grading system is one that considers (a) products of student performance, (b) processes that students use to complete their work, and (c) progress made on the classroom curriculum or individual learning objectives (Gersten et al., 1996).

In our research (Munk & Bursuck, 2001a; Munk et al., 2003), we have found that measuring and grading progress for students with disabilities often involves integrating the student's IEP objectives into the grading process. To do so requires a multistep process that warrants its own category, "Integrating the students' IEP into the grading process" (described in Chapter 8).

Returning to the conceptualization of a balanced grading system, "effort" has been isolated as a separate category from "processes." The rationale is simply that teachers have indicated that effort can and should be measured separately from processes that students use, such as using a strategy to solve math problems, because the students' competence with a process is influenced, at least in part, by external factors such as quality of instruction and access to tools.

Table 4 presents the three major areas in which student performance can be assessed and graded in the classroom areas of classwork, groupwork, homework, projects and tests/quizzes. Teachers generally assess student performances in two or more of these areas when determining report card grades.

Few readers will find this model of a balanced grading system provocative. In fact, such a model has been suggested for decades, and may even appear simplistic when compared to other models for grading in general education (e.g., Juarez, 1994). However, the model has proven effective for guiding teachers to better understand what they expect of their students, and how they could assess and grade their students' performances. To understand how the three areas can be "balanced," we must first understand precisely how each

(product, process, effort) fits into a grading system.

Products in the Balanced Grading System

The term "products" refers to permanent products generated by the student in completing an assignment. Long held to be valid evidence of student learning and achievement, common products include completed tests, reports, written papers, worksheets, or oral presentations. Obvious advantages of using products to determine grades for individual assignments or for a report card grade include (a) opportunity for ongoing assessment over time, (b) opportunity to observe progress as products are collected over time, (c) availability of evidence to share with the student and parents, and (d) opportunity to assess student performance "holistically," as in assessing a collection of student products in a portfolio.

In interactions with teachers in workshops and research projects, the author has encountered those who perceive grading student products as inherently less accurate or less fair for students with disabilities than their nondisabled peers because the students' problems with reading, comprehension, written expression, organization, and cognitive strategy use will ultimately lead to a product that

Table 4
Examples of Grades on Products, Processes and Effort in Six Common Areas of Expectation

Activity	Grade Products on	Grade Processes on	Grade Effort on...
Classwork	correct answers on worksheet completed individually	completing an organizer for writing assignment and then proofreading draft	• volunteering to answer question • attempting assignments
Groupwork	correct answers on single worksheet or lab report completed by a group	fulfilling assigned role in group	• participating in group • asking groupmates for help
Homework	percent of problems answered correctly	showing steps in completing a complex problem	attempting a certain number of problems
Projects	points earned on a rubric	following timeline and completing a checklist for project	• completing all parts of the project •getting help for problems
Tests/Quizzes	percent of correct answers	• following directions • drawing a picture to solve a problem	• answering a number of problems • asking to have directions clarified

is of lower quality, and hence a lower grade. Teachers expressing this perception are likely to view grading students based on processes and effort as desirable alternatives to products. To our knowledge, research has not specifically compared the relative benefits of emphasizing products, processes, or effort in a grading system.

It is important to remember that grading the products of students with disabilities should not affect the types and extent of curricular and instructional accommodations that are made for the student. In fact, a decision to emphasize products in your grading system magnifies the responsibility of the instructional staff to provide appropriate accommodations for test-taking (e.g., extra time, reading aloud to student), completing projects (e.g., assistive technology for reading and writing, timeline or project organizer), homework (e.g., modified assignment), or classwork (e.g., organizers or guided notes, individual assistance), per federal law.

Assuming that appropriate accommodations and supports are made for a student as the student completes assigned work, limitations on the accuracy of a grade for the student's products may remain. Two limitations include the inability of a product grade to capture and reflect how the student completed the work and the insensitivity of criteria for grading to capture the student's motivation and effort toward the work thus, the need for adjusting the balance of products, processes, and effort in the grading system.

Processes in the Balanced Grading System

In a nationwide survey on grading adaptations, general educators indicated that grading on the basis of process use, as well as productivity, was the most helpful adaptation (Bursuck et al., 1996). Given this level of support, we might expect a substantial research body on this type of adaptation. Curiously, few published articles have described grading of process use (Frierson, 1975; Horowitz, 1982).

In our 2001 study (Munk & Bursuck, 2001a), teachers implemented a grading adaptation in which one student, Jason, had 10% of his participation grade based on self-management of his portfolio for his social studies class. In our more recent study of personalized grading plans for 6th-grade included students with disabilities, more than 90% of the teams involved selected a grading adaptation that brought the student's use of processes into the grading system. Examples of the processes targeted in the personalized grading plans included self-management of project timelines, proofreading and editing strategies, solving math story problems using special strategies, and implementing a variety of strategies to improve reading comprehension (Munk et al., 2003).

No doubt we were all told by our teachers at one time or another to "show your work." The logic for such a request seemed obvious – the teacher wanted to see how we completed a task, often a math problem, to assess our knowledge of the steps or strategy to be followed. Typically, we were no longer required to "show our work" as we became proficient with the task. The treatment of processes in a balanced grading system has been influenced by the traditional definition of showing how a problem was solved, but is also based on current knowledge of interventions that help students with disabilities access and complete their work more efficiently.

Table 5 depicts three types of processes that students with disabilities are often expected to implement when pursuing their classroom work. Metacognitive or learning strategies, assistive technology, and self-management strategies are emphasized because the professional literature has shown the importance of these processes or tools for students, particularly those in upper elementary grades and above, who are included in general education settings. The author's experiences support the notion that students are being asked to use these processes, and that the appearance of processes related to strategy use, technology use, and self-management (as well as other "survival skills") in students' IEPs increases with age. Teachers are encouraged to consider the present description of processes as a guide, not an inclusive list, and to analyze their own assignments using the tools described in Chapter 7.

For teachers and administrators viewing Table 5, two insights may emerge. First, the relatively broad categories of learning strategies, technology use, and self-management might encompass a wide range of different strategies and devices. Furthermore, although the professional literature contains descriptions of techniques for teaching and encouraging students to use strategies and technological devices, most teachers want to "fit" a process to their students' particular strengths and needs. The extent to which processes are incorporated into a model for grading may depend on the knowledge and expertise of a student's teacher. Our experiences suggest great diversity in the knowledge and experiences of both general and special educators regarding learning and metacognitive strategies, instructional and assistive technologies, and self-management procedures. Therefore, we suggest that teams appraise their knowledge in these areas prior to considering adaptations that involve grading processes. Information regarding strategies and assistive technology can be found in textbooks, professional journals, college courses or workshops.

Fortunately, integrating processes into your balanced grading model may not require that you introduce processes to your students for the first time. Chances are that your students are already using some strategies to complete their work. In fact, they may even have IEP objectives

Table 5
Common Types of Processes Implemented by Students with Disabilities to Complete Work

Category	Description	Examples
Metacognitive or learning strategies to access curriculum and complete work	Student acquires, practices, and independently implements a strategy to improve performance of critical academic skills of reading, written expression, or math. Students may implement the strategy with a combination of covert (e.g., thinking) and overt (e.g., writing) steps.	Student uses a multistep strategy to paraphrase, illustrate, identify operation, write equation, and check the answer to a math word problem.
Instruction or assistive technologies to access curriculum and complete work	Student observes, practices and independently uses a technological device to enhance reading, written expression, math computation, oral communication, or physical manipulation of materials.	Student uses software that reads aloud as the student types an essay, allowing the student to listen and correct grammar and spelling.
Self-management procedures to organize, monitor, and complete work	Student develops, monitors, and evaluates own performance with a self-recording system (e.g., timeline, checklist).	Student completes a checklist that prompts the student to record homework assignment, check with teacher for understanding of assignment, and have parent initial completed homework.

that include strategy instruction by the teacher and strategy use by the student. We will describe an efficient procedure for identifying processes you may want to include in your balanced grading model in Chapter 7.

Potential advantages of including process use in your grading model extend to the student, parents, and teachers. For students, measuring and grading their use of processes may (a) increase their attention to processes because of the perceived increased importance, (b) increase the prominence of instruction on process use in their educational plan, (c) increase their use of processes that can be generalized to future work, and (d) produce assignment and report card grades that communicate how well they have used processes to complete their work.

For parents, measuring and grading their child's use of processes may: (a) provide information about the nature and extent of their child's disability and correlated needs in the general education classroom; (b) increase their attention to processes for which they might provide support, such as those used to complete homework; or (c) allow them to determine how well their child understands how to use processes that are designed to bypass or remediate the child's disability.

Finally, for teachers, incorporating processes into their grading model may: (a) improve services to their students; (b) increase their own knowledge and proficiency with learning strategies, technology use, and self-management procedures; and (c) allow them to recognize their students' progress or mastery of critical processes that may not be apparent in the products the students turn in for grading. This last point also represents a limitation of measuring and grading processes. That is, profi-

cient use of a process may not be reflected in a final product that is of lower quality. Indeed, a balance between product, process, and effort is required if a grading system is to be useful, accurate, and fair.

The Role of Effort in the Balanced Grading System

A suggestion to consider effort when assigning a grade to a student's work often evokes seemingly contradictory reactions from teachers. Many teachers are conflicted between wanting to acknowledge or even reward a student's effort, and wanting to be fair to all students. In fact, research suggests that assigning multiple grades, one reflecting effort, is perceived to be more fair than most other types of grading adaptations (Bursuck, Munk, & Olson, 1999) and is relatively more helpful to general educators (Bursuck et al., 1996). From another perspective, formed over several years of grading students, attempting to objectively measure effort is very difficult, and may leave a teacher open to questions of objectivity or fairness (Gersten et al., 1996).

Despite the obvious need to carefully and prudently incorporate effort into your balanced grading system, it is included in the present grading model because: (a) students, teachers, and parents regularly refer to effort when describing a student's performance, (b) our research suggests that many parents expect grades to communicate their child's effort (Munk & Bursuck, 2001b), (c) the level of a student's effort may give clues to why the student is or is not successful in the general education classroom regardless of the quality of supports being provided, and (d) the professional literature includes recommendations to consider effort (e.g., Lindsay, Burns, & Guthrie, 1984; Munk et al., 2003; Friedman & Truog, 1999).

The present model presents products, processes and effort as a unified grading system, rather than as individual areas for grading adaptations, because they are related areas that appear, formally or informally, in grading systems in most classrooms. A teacher who is pursuing a more effective way to assess and grade students may "adjust" the balance of the three areas for all students. Doing so may build in enough flexibility to accurately and fairly capture the performances of learners with different abilities and strengths. Although the primary focus of this book is to describe effective grading systems for students with disabilities, readers should be aware that any type of intervention that can be used with a whole class, rather than just select students, is more feasible and likely to be used consistently (Polloway,

Bursuck, Jayanthi, Epstein, & Nelson, 1996). Table 6 depicts how products, processes, and effort must be balanced to produce 100% of the emphasis in a grading system. The percentage of emphasis ascribed to these three areas must add up to 100% of the grading system. Therefore, teachers must balance the amounts of emphasis for each of the three components in a balanced grading system. This analogy of percentages of the grading system may be helpful for teams who are attempting to clarify or negotiate a grading system, because it illustrates that a grading system cannot accommodate high emphases on products, processes, and effort at the same time.

Grading adaptations that incorporate progress on IEP objectives.

Unlike the previously described categories of adaptations that may be implemented for all students, this category is unique to students who are eligible for special education services and, thus, have an Individualized Educational Program, or IEP. To receive a written IEP, a student must meet eligibility requirements for a disability based on federal and/or state criteria. The required components of IEPs for all students include (a) description of the student's present levels of performance, (b) measurable goals and objectives, (c) results of assessments, (d) rationale for any

Table 6
Balancing the Percentage of Emphasis on Product, Process and Effort in a Grading System

Area	Percentage of Grading System
Products	0% _____ 100%
Processes	0% _____ 100%
Effort	0% _____ 100%

time the student will spend in special settings away from nondisabled peers, (e) description of the services the student should receive, and (f) a description of how student progress will be reported. Readers interested in learning more about provisions of the Individuals with Disabilities Education Act (IDEA) and guidelines for constructing effective IEPs are encouraged to read Bateman and Linden's (1998) comprehensive text on these topics.

The strategy of incorporating a measure of student progress on IEP objectives into a grading system has received anecdotal support in the professional literature for decades (e.g., Cohen, 1983; Frierson, 1975); however, studies evaluating procedures or outcomes for this grading adaptation have not been advanced. Teachers have also reported grading

on progress on IEP objectives as being relatively helpful compared to other types of grading adaptations (Bursuck et al., 1996).

Two components of the IEP, measurable goals and objectives, and progress monitoring, are related to grading and can be adapted to meet the needs of an individual student. This chapter will focus on the adaptation of grading based on progress on IEP objectives. A later chapter will discuss how progress can be monitored and reported in a chapter dedicated to those specific topics (Chapter 11).

A student's IEP must contain annual goals, each with benchmarks or short-term objectives that describe intermediate steps or milestones to be reached on the way to meeting the annual goal. Learning objectives or benchmarks include student performance that is measurable, an obvious requirement if progress is to be used for grading purposes.

Given that all students' IEPs contain goals and objectives, one might expect that basing all or part of their grades on progress on objectives might be straight forward and widely used. However, precise guidelines for when to use IEP objectives for grading have not been advanced. A rationale for using any type of grading adaptation should include its potential benefit to the student's current and future performance, as defined by the student, parents, and school personnel. When objectives focus on improvement in critical foundation skills such as reading fluency and comprehension, written expression, oral communication, or mathematical computation or problem solving, the case for potential benefit is easily made. Whether or not to incorporate progress on such objectives into the grading system for a student may be based on (a) the degree to which the student's progress on the objective will directly affect performances on the classroom curriculum, (b) the degree to which progress on the objective will allow the student to function more independently in the general education classroom and curriculum, and (c) the amount of emphasis, time, and effort placed on the IEP objective by the student's team.

Imagine a 5th-grader, Woody, whose IEP includes an annual goal and short term objectives for improving comprehension of expository texts (textbooks). Assuming that Woody has learned to use several strategies (e.g., summarizations, retell, graphic organizer) to facilitate comprehension when he reads, his progress in effectively using his strategies could be worthy of integration into his grading system for the social studies class. Improving his comprehension as he reads the materials in the class will improve his performance with all class materials and assignments, presumably in all context areas. Furthermore, Woody would be able to function more independently and rely less on the special educator to review the materials and ask him questions. Lastly, informing Woody that part of his grade will be based on how well he uses his comprehension strategies may motivate him, as well as his teachers, to continue practicing strategy use.

Thus far we have attempted to describe how progress on an IEP objective can be integrated into the grading system, as well as why or when a team would consider such a grading adaptation. Never consider an IEP objective "worthy" of use for grading purposes unless it meets the following assumptions. To do so would undermine any potential benefit to the student.

1. The objective focuses on a skill that will benefit the student in the student's current classes.

2. The objective is currently written or could be revised to include a method for measuring progress.

3. Ample opportunities for working on the objective will be available in the general education classroom.

Additional detail on how to incorporate progress into the grading system will be provided in Chapter 7.

Grading adaptations that involve measuring improvement.

The fourth category of grading adaptations involves basing all or part of an assignment or report card grade on improvement over past performances. Examples of adaptations in this category might include boosting a student's grade, perhaps by adding "bonus points" if the student improves performance by a specified amount. For example, a teacher may offer to increase a student's quiz score by 2 points if the student can increase his scores by 10 points on three consecutive quizzes. The adaptation of using improvement as a basis for grading has been described in the professional literature for three decades (e.g., Frierson, 1975; Lieberman, 1982; Slavin, 1980; Zoboroski, 1981), and seems best suited as a strategy to

motivate students to work hard and improve their performance. Indeed, general education teachers have reported that grading on improvement is one of the most helpful adaptations (Bursuck et al., 1996). In our recent research on personalized grading plans, adaptations that involved grading improvement in asking questions in class and completing homework were selected for 6th graders with disabilities (Munk et al., 2003).

For students receiving low grades, adding emphasis and weight to improvement may provide an incentive to pursue higher grades, even when those grades are still considered "low." Grading on improvement may seem a rather straightforward procedure–assess current performance and establish goals for improvement. However, it is more complicated in that improvement can be measured in performances on products, process use, effort, and IEP objectives, thus, overlapping with adaptations in those areas. In fact, teachers may want to consider grading on improvement in addition to other grading adaptations, with the increase in focus on improvement serving as an incentive for the student to participate in the other adaptations.

Grading on improvement does present some obvious limitations. One potential limitation is that a student's improvement may be beneficial only to the extent that what is achieved is beneficial. Therefore, working to get a higher grade should correspond to increased learning of important content, not just a higher grade. Educators must be certain to target important knowledge and skills when introducing grading on improvement. A second limitation might be that the amount of improvement that is prescribed will still leave the student well behind classmates. Consequently, educators must be certain to set criteria for improvement at a level that will produce benefits to the student, even if the improvement is incremental over time. For example, even if a student who has a goal for increasing homework completion by 30% for one marking period, meets this goal, the result may only be 60% of homework completed, and a failing grade in that area.

Another limitation is that a student's performance may not improve because: (a) grades do not function as rewards for the student, or (b) the student does not possess the knowledge and skill to improve the student's performance. In response to teachers who describe the first scenario, a student who "couldn't care less about grades," we encourage the teachers to go ahead and grade improvement, with careful attention to the response of the student and parents as they observe how improve-

ment affects the grade. Our experiences suggest that some students do "care" about their grades even though they will not say as much when discussing grades with their teachers. The latter problem of a student not having the capabilities or resources to improve performance must be taken seriously because of the potentially harmful effects of encouraging a student who will work hard but ultimately perform poorly due to lack of knowledge and skill. As teachers, we sometimes categorize student performance problems as "can't versus won't." Teams must make sure that a student can improve performance before offering the incentive of potentially higher grades.

We will describe procedures for effective implementation of adaptations involving improvement in Chapter 9.

Grading adaptations that involve changing scales and weights.

This fifth, and final, category includes adaptations that involve changes to the scales used to assign a specified letter grade (e.g., A, B, C, D, F), or weights assigned to different types of expectations for determining a report card grade (e.g., test grades or total points on tests count as 60% of report card grade). Changing the scale for grades has been reported in the professional literature

(Drucker & Hansen, 1982) and has been implemented frequently by teachers in our research projects (Munk & Bursuck, 2001a; Munk et al., 2003). Arbitrarily assigning weights to assignments has been cited as a problem in grading systems for general education students (Marzano, 2000).

Teachers seem to have different opinions of the two adaptations in this category. That is, changing weights assigned to assignments is perceived as somewhat helpful, whereas changing the grading scale is not considered very helpful (Bursuck et al., 1996). In our research, the rationale given for this type of adaptation is often that the existing grading scale is "punishing" or "unfair" to some students with disabilities because no matter how hard they try, or how many supports they receive, they will never earn a grade that they consider satisfactory or fair. When this scenario is repeated over several marking periods, a student may become disillusioned and "give up."

To prevent this from happening, the teacher may adjust the grading scale so that a student can earn a higher grade by continuing to perform at the same level. One obvious potential benefit of changing the grading scale is that a student may be motivated to try hard. Although not proven by research, motivational benefit may be greater for a student who stands to move from a D to a B with a change in the grading scale than for one who stands to move from an F to a D. Changing scales or weights can be used to "jump start" students who have become disillusioned due to a history of negative feedback and low or failing grades.

Despite its potential for increasing student motivation and its relative ease in implementation, changing the grading scale does possess a downside that warrants highlighting. Changing the grading scale does not "individualize" a grading system in the same manner as the previous adaptations we have discussed. That is, changing the scale does not increase attention to a student's specific strengths or challenges, nor does it involve individual learning objectives. Changing the scale suggests that a student's current level of performance is acceptable, and that the supports that are being provided are adequate. Obviously, concerns about this adaptation exist, and it is recommended only when a team is convinced that the above conditions have been met.

When it comes to the issues surrounding changing weights of assignments, the concerns are somewhat different. That is, the standards for student performance remain the same, only the amount of weight that a specific type of assignment (e.g., projects) counts toward the report card grade is changed. Shifting weights from one type of expectation (e.g., tests) to another (e.g., homework) may be best used when a student's learning can be evidenced through assignments that do not interact as strongly with the student's disability. The most frequently observed adaptation in this regard is shifting of weight from tests/quizzes to performance areas that allow the student to use as much time as needed to complete assigned work, such as projects or homework. As is the case for changing scales, teams should consider changing weights only if they are convinced that a student's learning may be assessed accurately in other performance areas to which weight is shifted.

We present procedures for effective implementation of adaptations involving changes to scale or weights in Chapter 10.

Differentiating Adaptations from Alternatives to Grading

In previous discussions of grading adaptations (Bursuck & Friend, 2001; Munk & Bursuck, 1998a, 1998b) we included alternative systems to letter grades – pass-fail and competency checklists. In a pass-fail system, criteria are developed for receiving a pass or a fail grade on an assignment or a report card. Advocates of this system suggest that it relieves pressure on students to earn a high grade and may increase students' focus on learning (Durm, 1993; Haladnya, 1999). For students with disabilities, the effects of receiving low grades on a consistent basis may thwart their motivation; hence they may welcome a system that does not require grades. While these potential benefits are very attractive, they may not overshadow the fact that nearly all schools use a letter/number grading system, and that many postsecondary institutions and employers expect graduates to have a grading record and a GPA. In fact, in some states, the use of alternative grading systems may affect a student's eligibility for graduation and may affect the type of diploma the student can earn. Thus, the decision to use any alternative to letter/number grades must be done cautiously and with an eye to the student's postsecondary plans.

The other alternative to letter/number grades, competency checklists, offer the same benefits and limitations as the pass-fail system. However, an additional advantage of the competency checklist is that is provides very detailed information on the student's performance to the student and the student's parents. Thus, competency checklists may be used in conjunction with grades to provide desired information on the student's performance.

Another perspective on alternatives to letter/number systems is that they may deprive a student with a disability from participating in the same grading system as typical peers (Chandler, 1983; Lieberman, 1983). The right to participate in the "typical" grading system, even when there is a risk of receiving low grades, should be upheld for students with disabilities. Perhaps by insisting that their children participate in the typical grading systems in their schools, parents of students with disabilities will promulgate changes in the systems that will benefit all students, including those with disabilities.

Chapter Summary

This chapter described five commonly used types of grading adaptations for which support exists in the professional literature. Each type of adaptation "functions" in a different way, or serves a different purpose; thus, it is important that teachers be familiar with all types of adaptations when considering one for an individual student. The intended message of this chapter was that "one size does not fit all" when it comes to grading adaptations.

Suggested Activities

The following activities are suggested for learning more about the topic of grading adaptations or for getting started on changes to your current grading system:

- Consider what types of grading adaptations you are currently using, perhaps informally, for students in your classroom. Are you using adaptations effectively? Are there types of adaptations that you are not currently using, but that might benefit a student in your class?

- Discuss the use of grading adaptations with your colleagues. When doing so, make sure that the setting is one in which everyone feels comfortable sharing and that they are not concerned that they might get into trouble for using "unofficial" grading practices. It may help to start the conversation by saying that the research suggests that many teachers make grading adaptations for their students with and without disabilities.

- Review your school's grading policy for evidence that specific types of adaptations are encouraged or allowed. Most policies do not contain information about grading adaptations. If yours does not, you may suggest that a committee work on revising it.

- Review the types of background knowledge needed to make certain types of grading adaptations. For example, grading adaptations involving the grading of process use require knowledge of the types of strategies, technology, or self management strategies that students can use. If you would like to gain more knowledge in these areas, you might ask a colleague or seek out reading materials on these topics. Grading adaptations involving prioritization require that you adopt a criterion for prioritizing. If you are not familiar with the learning standards for your school, or the requirements for upper level classes in your content area, you may want to talk with an experienced colleague or contact the curriculum director for your district.

Where Do We Go From Here?

This lengthy chapter has presented different types of grading adaptations available to teachers and emphasized the potential strengths of each adaptation. To this point, the book has described issues that warrant use of grading adaptations and how to select a grading adaptation by clarifying the purpose for grades. This chapter has presented the "menu" of grading adaptations from which teachers must choose. The next chapter will present a process and tool for evaluating a grading adaptation and deciding if it meets a student's needs.

CHAPTER 5
Evaluating Grading Adaptations

This chapter will present criteria and procedures for evaluating each of the types of grading adaptations described in Chapter 4. An evaluation tool and procedure is necessary because no single grading adaptation can meet everyone's expectations, and all possess some limitation that must be considered. Thus, some thought and analysis must go into selecting a grading adaptation, and no adaptation will be implemented the same way or have the same effect for any two students.

The natural reaction of any conscientious teacher presented with a menu of strategies is to look for guidance in selecting the best option. Sources of guidance include research findings, recommendations from "experts," the shared knowledge and experience of colleagues, and the student's preferences. Indeed, for children in upper-elementary to high school, asking them how they should be graded is a necessary step in se-

lecting an appropriate grading adaptation. For teachers who prefer to base their decisions on solid research that can be generalized to a broad array of students and classrooms, the recommended approach to evaluating grading adaptations may be frustrating, in that it relies heavily on decision-making by teachers or teams. Such reactions may seem logical, but readers should recognize that all decisions about grading must be based on a number of different factors, many of which require knowledge of the student and collaborative, team-based decision making.

Taking a slightly different angle on the issue of flexibility and teamwork, and readers are cautioned who prefer discussing philosophical, political, and policy aspects of grading that the point of evaluating potential grading adaptations is to identify the best fit with the team's goals for the student, and to "observe for evidence" that an adaptation is working. Thus the strategy for developing an effective grading system involves moving from a discussion of abstract concepts such as fairness, to concrete, observable procedures such as recording how many steps in a writing strategy a student completed correctly.

The disparate ratio of discussion to research articles was discussed earlier and the number of difficult to control factors that influence the development and use of a grading system appear overwhelming to prospective researchers. In the remainder of this chapter we will describe several criteria for evaluating the potential benefits of a grading adaptation, and provide a tool for recording the potential benefit of each adaptation. Our expectation is that teachers or teams will complete the evaluation process in a deliberate fashion in the beginning, but will spend less time on evaluating as they become more familiar with the criteria. In the process, teachers may also identify additional criteria for evaluating grading adaptations. For example, the time and effort required to implement a grading adaptation can influence its attractiveness. Teachers who have implemented grading adaptations will have a sense of the time and effort required and can informally calculate a cost-benefit ratio for a particular adaptation.

Table 7 depicts an evaluation matrix we have developed for evaluating different types of grading adaptations. The items on the evaluation form are intended to represent desirable characteristics for an adaptation, and reflect what teachers or teams want to achieve by pursuing a grading adaptation.

In most cases, the desirable characteristics represent the opposing form of one of the issues discussed in Chapter 2. For example, item 5 addresses collaboration between parents and teachers in developing and implementing a grading system for a child. Absence of such collaboration is a recognized problem; thus, the potential to improve collaboration would be a desirable characteristic for a grading adaptation. Other items, such as 1 and 4, address important issues related to grading. Adaptations that are likely to promote access by the student to the general education curriculum, or increase the extent to which a student's learning objectives on the IEP are addressed in the general education classroom, are generally desirable for students with mild disabilities in general education classrooms.

The complexity of factors to consider when selecting or developing a grading adaptation are further evidenced in the criteria selected for

Table 7
Grading Adaptations Evaluation Matrix

Characteristic	Description	Probable	Possible	Requires Special Attention
Effect on the Grade				
1. Produces grades that accurately reflect progress on general education curriculum.	Student's performance on the classroom curriculum is emphasized. Student is provided access to maximum amount of curriculum and is encouraged to master as much as possible.			
2. Produces grades that accurately reflect student effort and motivation.	Student effort is isolated, measured and translated into a grade.			
3. Produces grades that accurately reflect progress on individual or IEP learning goals.	Particular IEP objectives are addressed in the general education classroom. A system for measuring progress and translating it to a grade is developed.			
4. Produces grades that will motivate student to try hard in the future.	Grading adaptation is sensitive to incremental improvements in performance.			
Effect on the Grading Process				
5. Results in collaboration between teachers and parents.	Adaptation requires input and follow-through from teachers and parents.			

Table 7 (continued)

Characteristic	Description	Probable	Possible	Requires Special Attention
<u>Effect on the Grading Process</u>				
6. Results in collaboration between special and general educators.	Adaptation requires teachers to work together to plan, monitor, and evaluate.			
7. Results in coordination of the classroom accommodations and how the student is graded.	Team considers all accommodations when designing adaptation. How accommodations are selected may be influenced by how the student will be graded.			
8. Results in access to the general education curriculum.	To implement the adaptation, the teachers will provide maximum access to classroom curriculum and student will complete all or most of assignments.			
<u>Effect on Community Perspectives</u>				
9. Perceived as fair by typical classmates.	Adaptaion is based on student need and does not involve rewarding student for no work or effort.			
10. Perceived as fair by other teachers.	Adaptation based on student need and does not involve rewarding for no work or effort.			

evaluating adaptations. Note that the three categories from which to choose include: Probable, Possible, or Requires Special Attention. By "Probable," we mean the procedures that the team would follow to select, develop, implement, and monitor a particular adaptation would likely result in achieving a particular characteristic. For example, a grading adaptation that involves prioritization of the classroom content and related assignments based on the district's learning standards is likely to achieve characteristic 1: "Produce grades that accurately reflect progress on the general education curriculum." Therefore, we would mark Probable for item 1 on the evaluation matrix. We would also mark Probable for item 8: "Result in access to the general education curriculum." Aside from these two items, we may not mark Probable for any other characteristics, although all may be achieved. For example, the general and special educator may collaborate to prioritize the content for the classroom (item 6) and other teachers may indeed perceive the adaptation as very fair (item 10). Because these characteristics could be achieved with minimal special effort, we would mark Possible for each item. With regard to item 2: "Produce grades that accurately reflect student effort and motivation," it is less clear how this characteristic can be achieved by prioritizing the classroom

content. Perhaps if the student were involved in the prioritization process, the student might be expected to be more motivated to work hard. But this represents an unpredictable scenario that would have to be arranged by the teachers. Therefore, we would mark the box labeled "Requires Special Attention."

Once a teacher or team has evaluated one or more potential grading adaptations, they will proceed quickly to interpreting their results and making a final decision on whether to adopt a particular adaptation or adaptations. Here again, no formula or cutoff score can predict whether an individual adaptation will generate enough benefit to warrant the time it will take for implementation. The author's experience suggests that the process of identifying, selecting, and developing a grading adaptation for a particular student is best completed through face to face discussion among team members of the pros and cons of different adaptations.

We recommend that teams employ techniques commonly used for group problem solving, such as generating and evaluating potential solutions (Friend & Cook, 1996). It is especially important that the team consider the positives and negatives for each adaptation. Positive aspects might include the presence of more than one of the desirable characteristics described in Table 7. Ease of implementation and generalizablity of an adaptation to different classes might also be considered positive attributes. Adaptations with few negative attributes have been presented; however, teachers may perceive some adaptations to be more time-consuming than others, and thus less attractive.

A Close Look at "Fairness"

The last section of the evaluation tool (Effects on Community Perspectives) prompts consideration of how other students and colleagues will judge fairness of a grading adaptation for a particular student. Sources for our discussion of the fairness of grading adaptations include our own research, as well as published works on a theoretical perspective at fairness.

In a national survey of 368 elementary and secondary regular education teachers, Bursuck et al. (1996) investigated the perceived usefulness and fairness of grading adaptations. Findings relevant to the present discussion showed that 73% of respondents felt that making grading adaptations for only students with disabilities was unfair. This finding may be related to the wording of the survey item because most teachers added that they perceived a problem with making adaptations for some, but not all students. Thus, their response was not a reflection of whether they thought individual types of adaptations are more or less fair. Clearly, the respondents were concerned about not making grading adaptations for all students.

Bursuck et al. (1999) investigated student perceptions of the fairness of grading adaptations by surveying 254 students in grades 9 - 12 who were grouped into four GPA categories based on the schools 4-point scale: low (GPA below 2.0), low-average (GPA 2.0 - 2.99), high-average (3.0 - 3.74), and high (3.74 - 4.55) (GPAs over 4.0 resulted from honors points). A fifth group of respondents consisted of students with learning disabilities. Participating students were asked to rate nine different grading adaptations as fair or unfair. Table 8 presents the nine grading adaptations, how the overall group rated them, and any differences by achievement level. As illustrated, all of the adaptations were rated as being more unfair than fair. In a series of open-ended questions, students were asked to specify which adaptations were most and least fair. Grading adaptations perceived as most fair, and the percentage of students indicating so, were as follows:

- Higher report card grade for doing their best (21.9%)

Table 8
Summary of Results: Student Perceptions of Grading Adaptations

Grading Adaptation	Fair	Not Fair	Differences Between Achievement Levels
Give some students a higher report card grade because they show improvement.	36	220	judged as more fair by students with learning disabilities
Give some students two grades for each subject (one for how hard they tried and one for how well they did).	117	159	
Change how much certain things count towards the report card grades of some students (for example, make assigments worth more than tests).	91	164	judged as more fair by students with learning disabilities
Give some students a higher report card grade when they do the best they can.	113	143	
Give some students a report card grade based on having to learn less material.	47	206	
Grade some students using a different scale.	34	222	judged as more fair by students with learning disabilities
Give some students a passing report card grade, no matter what.	13	242	
Pass some students no matter how poorly they do (as long as they try hard).	62	193	
Grade some students on a pass-fail basis (without using letter or number grades).	88	167	judged as more fair by students with learning disabilities

Source: Bursuck, W. D., Munk, D. D., & Olson, M. M. (1999). The fairness of report card grading adaptations: What do students with and without disabilities think? *Remedial and Special Education, 20,* 84-92. Reprinted with permission of Pro-Ed, Inc.

- None of the adaptations was fair (17.8%)

- Give two grades, one for performance, one for effort (17.8%)

- Pass students as long as they try hard (13.7%)

Obviously, even adaptations perceived as more fair still received relatively little support, and the second-highest comment was that none of the adaptations was fair. Following are the grading adaptations perceived as least fair by the students:

- Pass students no matter what (27.60%)

- Grade students using a different scale (18.40%)

- All of the adaptations were unfair (13.16%)

- Grade on a pass-fail basis (11.84%)

In the two studies on perceived fairness of grading adaptations, the following themes seem evident:

1. Teachers and students may judge an adaptation as more or less fair depending on whether it is available to all students, not just to some students. Thus, the degree to which a teacher uses all or part of an adaptation for an entire class may influence perceived fairness. If 50% of teachers are making informal adaptations for students without disabilities (Bursuck et al., 1996), then some adaptations may be available to most or all students.

2. Grading adaptations in which the student's effort or maximizing of potential is considered may be perceived as relatively more fair.

3. Students with disabilities and those who are low achieving are likely to view a broader range of grading adaptations as fair.

At this point, you may be questioning encouragement to implement a type of intervention that may be perceived as unfair by both students and colleagues. In fact, the findings in these studies are not surprising in that similar viewpoints regarding instructional and curricular modifications for disabilities have been voiced for years. Given that grades and GPAs function as the currency in the economy of post secondary institutions, is it any wonder that teachers and students are sensitive to issues of fairness? Regardless, teams must acknowledge concerns about fairness and take whatever steps are possible to promote fairness in all aspects of classroom life. Understanding what "fairness" may mean to each individual student is a good start to promoting it in your classroom. The topic will be introduced with a scenario depicting the effects of different perceptions of fairness.

The Case of Chandra and Cliff

Chandra and Cliff are both in Mrs. Grevey's 5th-grade social studies class. They are neighbors and friends, and share everything that happens at school. Today is report card day, and Cliff is quick to show Chandra that he got an A in social studies. But Chandra gets a funny look on her face when she sees Cliff's grade. Then she proceeds to say that she also got an A, and that she does all her own work, while Cliff gets help because he has an IEP. Chandra says, "Even though you are my friend, I don't think it's fair that we got the same grade because you get to have the tests read to you and you get more time to do the tests. Also, you get extra points for trying hard even though no one else gets points for trying." Cliff is stunned and hurt at his friend's remarks, and runs ahead of Chandra to get home.

Defining "Fairness"

Chandra's reaction to the accommodations being made for Cliff are not unusual. In fact, they are actually logical if we consider the definitions of fairness described by Welch (2000). Following is a brief description and example for each of the three definitions.

Maintaining equality: When fairness is defined as equality, all students receive the same reward simply because they are part of the class. When applied to the example of an inclusive classroom, equality would mean that all students receive the same amount of attention from the teacher, opportunities for certain kinds of work, and the same grading criteria. When fairness is defined as equality, the strengths or needs of an individual student do not necessarily result in more reward for that student.

Maintaining Equity: When fairness is defined as equity, students receive a reward that is proportionate to their input or performance. When applied to the example of an inclusive classroom, equity would mean that students who get the most math problems correct, or write the best essay, receive more reward in the forms of teacher attention and higher grades. Conversely, students who, because of their disability, receive shortened assignments are eligible for a lower grade than their typical peers. When fairness is defined as equity, it may be difficult for students with disabilities to capture teacher attention or other rewards available in the classroom.

Meeting needs: When fairness is defined as meeting a student's needs, students receive rewards according to their needs. When applied to the example of an inclusive classroom, students with disabilities may receive ample teacher attention and supports because they need the extra support to be successful. Their teachers may also make adaptations to the grading process so that the students with disabilities are able to earn passing or high grades.

Influencing Students' Perspectives

Helping students shift from a perspective that fairness requires equality or equity, to one in which fairness may mean meeting an individual's needs requires both sensitivity and judgment. Welch (2000) offers the following suggestions:

- Teach the different types of fairness early in the school year and without reference to any particular student or issue.

- Check to see if a student's concerns about fairness are really a request for more individual attention from the teacher.

- Respond consistently to a students' concerns by asking if they would like the teacher to do something for them.

- Create opportunities in which you can give special attention or privileges to all students in the classroom.

- Treat student concerns with respect and provide a way for students to register complaints.

The process for implementing grading adaptations for included students requires ongoing communication between the student, parents, general educator, and special educator. Many issues must be considered when selecting the appropriate adaptation to meet a student's needs. Table 7 offers an evaluation matrix that includes 10 potentially beneficial characteristics of a grading adaptation. Readers are urged to consider each of the characteristics, as well as using any additional criteria that you can identify, when planning a change in your grading system.

Chapter Summary

This chapter described one method and tool for evaluating different types of grading adaptations on a variety of criteria. Although the criteria included in the evaluation tool were based on the most prominent issues described in Chapter 2, they are by no means exclusive. Teachers will want to add other criteria that they deem important (e.g., time requirements to make the adaptation).

This chapter also included a discussion of the perceived fairness of grading adaptations. Concerns about fairness are inevitable whenever different procedures are used for some, but not all students. Rather than avoid using grading adaptations because students may complain about fairness, teachers are encouraged to address the issue of fairness directly by using one of the strategies described in this chapter.

Suggested Activities

The following activities are suggested for learning more about grading adaptations or fairness, or for getting started on making changes to your current grading system:

• Start a discussion about general issues of fairness at your team or department meeting. Make sure that the setting is considered "safe" by everyone, so that no one is afraid to speak frankly. It is important to point out that fairness is valued in our society, and one should not feel bad about questioning whether making adaptations for one student is unfair to others. Only by respecting everyone's opinion will you achieve a productive conversation.

• Implement one or more of the adaptations and keep notes on the criteria you use to judge its effectiveness. For example, you might record evidence for improved communication, improved student learning, or increased focus on the student's IEP objectives. Consider other criteria that you might use, but that are not listed on the evaluation tool.

• Identify a grading adaptation that you or a colleague are making right now. Evaluate the adaptation using the tool included in this chapter and then consider whether the adaptation is providing enough potential benefit, or if you can modify it to meet more of the criteria.

Where Do We Go From Here?

The first five chapters presented the case for making grading adaptations for included students with disabilities. At this point, you are familiar with the types of grading adaptations and the criteria you might use to select an adaptation to fit your students' needs and the expectations of the entire team. The next five chapters will describe specific procedures for implementing each of the types of grading adaptations.

SECTION 3
Implementing Grading Adaptations

CHAPTER 6
Prioritizing Content and
Related Assignments

This chapter will describe the following procedures for implementing grading adaptations based on prioritization of content and related assignments:

• Identifying guidelines or standards for prioritizing content

• Ranking your content by importance

• Determining how content will be covered and graded

Choosing Guidelines or Standards

In general, the classroom teacher makes decisions about what content will be taught and how student learning will be assessed. This responsibility, right, or privilege is a hallmark of classroom teaching that is valued by most teachers, and allows for some degree of originality or personalization of classroom instruction. Thus,

two teachers who cover the same content are likely to place emphases on different units of the content because they have different perceptions of what is most important. For example, two social studies teachers may be following the same standards and using the same textbook and materials for their U.S. history class. However, one of them may perceive the historical events that led to the Civil War to be most important for students to learn because it exemplifies the tension between centralized versus regional and state interests and governance, while a colleague may perceive the period of Reconstruction as the most important because of its role in the shaping of our country following the war. Informally, both teachers have prioritized their content based on perceived importance, and each has likely spent more time and thought preparing for content they perceive as more important. Both teachers cover the necessary content to meet the standards, but they tend to place more emphasis on assignments that address their own "prioritized" content.

Prioritization of content by the classroom teacher is not only common, but advantageous when developing a grading system that is equitable for all learners in an inclusive classroom. When you can prioritize your content, you can decide how to develop assignments and a grading process that focuses on the important content for your class. By prioritizing first, you will avoid spending planning, instructing, and grading time on relatively less important content and related assignments.

Before you can prioritize the content for your class, you must decide what criteria you will use to rank the content by importance. For better or for worse, no precise guidelines exist for prioritizing the content; therefore, you must identify a criterion upon which to base your prioritization. We suggest that you consider the following influences:

Learning Standards: Should you prioritize content that is directly related to learning standards for your state, district, or professional organization?

Local curriculum: Should you prioritize content that is most directly related to your school's curriculum?

Prerequisite skills: Should you prioritize content that helps students develop prerequisite skills for more advanced classes?

Relevance to students' lives: Should you prioritize content that you think has more relevance to the students' everyday lives?

No doubt you recognize the four influences described above, and have already decided which you believe is most helpful for prioritizing your curriculum. For many teachers, the decision of which influence to follow may not be theirs to make, at least not entirely. As this point in time, the practice of "standards-based" education is being promoted throughout the country, and schools are developing or adopting learning standards upon which to base instruction (King-Sears, 2001).

The increased emphasis on standards-based education is driven by the perception that adhering to clearly defined standards will improve student performance and increase the accountability for teachers and schools (Thurlow, 2002). Related to the push for standards-based instruction is an increased emphasis on "high-stakes" assessments that presumably assess student learning, and that are linked in content to a specified set of learning standards. Thus, students who receive instruction that is anchored in the learning standards should perform better on high-stakes assessments. A related issue that is relevant to this discussion is language in IDEA (1997) indicating that students with disabilities must be included in the same schoolwide assessments as their peers without disabilities, or a rationale must be given for conducting an alternative assessment that addresses student performance on similar content (Thompson, Quenemoen, Thurlow, & Ysseldyke, 2001). Together, the practices of standards-based instruction and inclusion of all students in large scale assessments have created an atmosphere in inclusive education in which providing maximum exposure and access to the general education curriculum for students with disabilities is highly valued (Pugach & Warger, 2001). Given this emphasis, you should base your prioritization on the learning standards for your district first, and then on other influences if further prioritization is warranted.

How to Prioritize

The Planning Pyramid (Schumm, Vaughn, & Harris, 1997) is a helpful tool for prioritizing the expectations for an inclusive classroom. The sample pyramid depicted in Figure 3 has been completed for a science unit on cells.

The top of the pyramid represents the smaller amount of information or content the teachers expect only some, probably higher achieving students, to learn. This means that while all or most students in the class will participate in instruction on this content, only a few of them are likely to master the information with "typical" instruction, which includes accommodations for students with disabilities.

The middle level of the pyramid represents the content or information that the teachers expect most students to master. Based on the prior performances and known abilities of the students in the class, the teachers anticipate that most students will be able to master the information or content in this level with "typical" instruction, including accommodations for students with disabilities.

Finally, the base level of the pyramid contains the information or content that the teachers anticipate all or most students will learn.

The primary materials for the unit depicted in Figure 3 will be a published textbook. To complete the pyramid, the science and special education teachers first determined that all of the content to be covered would address learning standards for the state and local district. Thus, they chose to prioritize the content based on prerequisite skills for a more advanced class. The content that they

Figure 3
The Planning Pyramid: Example for a Science Unit on Cells

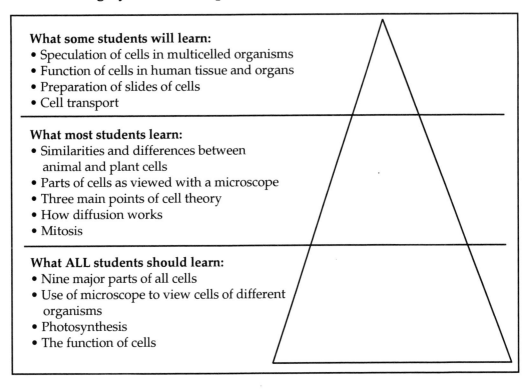

What some students will learn:
• Speculation of cells in multicelled organisms
• Function of cells in human tissue and organs
• Preparation of slides of cells
• Cell transport

What most students learn:
• Similarities and differences between animal and plant cells
• Parts of cells as viewed with a microscope
• Three main points of cell theory
• How diffusion works
• Mitosis

What ALL students should learn:
• Nine major parts of all cells
• Use of microscope to view cells of different organisms
• Photosynthesis
• The function of cells

perceived as vital to future learning in science was placed at the bottom of the pyramid to indicate that it was to be learned by all students. Content that was vital and would be learned by most, but not all students, was placed in the middle level of the pyramid. Last, more complex content that would be mastered by a few students, and that would be most useful for advanced science content, was placed at the top of the pyramid. Note that the placement of the content on the pyramid was based on the judgments of the teachers; you may have prioritized the information differently. If so, ask yourself what criteria you are using to prioritize content.

The authors of the Planning Pyramid emphasize that prioritizing content should not result in reduced expectations or access for students with disabilities. Rather, prioritizing is an acknowledgment that not all students will learn everything that is covered in a class; therefore, teachers in an inclusive classroom will want to plan instruction so as to provide ample time and support to students on content at all three levels of the pyramid. In brief, prioritizing helps the special educator make decisions about how best to support the included student.

The link between prioritizing content and grading is obvious: We want to develop a grading process that captures and communicates student performance on content that has been given higher priority. The following tool allows teachers to prioritize curriculum for a marking period and to identify the expectations in which the curriculum will be addressed. Tool 6-1 has been completed collaboratively by the same educators and for the same content as described in Figure 3. However, note that the content has been prioritized as 1 - 6 within Tool 6-1. In addition, it provides a checklist of expectations matched with the content that will be encountered by the student. Aligning the prioritized content with classroom expectations is an important step in deciding how to support students with disabilities. With the information from Tool 6-1, the team can observe what will be taught and what expectations will be placed on students in the class.

The Planning Pyramid and Tool 6-1 lend themselves well to prioritizing content over individual lessons or units. Thus, the general and special educator would be required to complete the process periodically throughout a marking period and over a school year. While readers may not see the repetition of this process as an extraordinary burden, especially since clarifying what will be taught ahead of time will help both teachers plan for the whole class, there may be cases in which you may want to plan for a longer period of time.

In our research, we have asked teachers to forecast their planned instruction and grading system for an entire marking period, usually 9-12 weeks. Once they have done so, they may choose to prioritize within individual units or lessons if needed for a grading system for a particular student. Tool 6-2 is designed to help you prioritize your content for a marking period or longer. To use the tool, you simply list the content you plan to cover in order of perceived importance. The checklist in the second column allows you to indicate what criteria will be important when collaborating with the student, parents, and colleagues. The third column contains another checklist of classroom areas of expectation in which the student will access the content and be assessed.

Tips from Teachers
Teachers who have participated in our research projects have sug-

Tool 6-1
Clarifying Prioritized Content and How It Will Be Assessed

Prioritized Content	Expectation Areas in Which Primarily Assessed for Grading	
Most Important	Check all that apply	
1. Identify nine major parts of all cells.	_X_ classwork ____ projects _X_ tests/quizzes	_X_ homework _X_ groupwork
2. Use a microscope to view cells of different organisms.	_X_ classwork _X_ projects ____ tests/quizzes	____ homework ____ groupwork
3. Describe the stages in photosynthesis.	_X_ classwork ____ projects _X_ tests/quizzes	_X_ homework _X_ groupwork
4. Describe the functions of cells.	_X_ classwork ____ projects _X_ tests/quizzes	_X_ homework _X_ groupwork
5. Describe the similarities and differences between cells of animals and plants.	_X_ classwork _X_ projects _X_ tests/quizzes	____ homework ____ groupwork
6. Identify parts of cells as viewed under a microscope.	_X_ classwork _X_ projects ____ tests/quizzes	____ homework ____ groupwork

gested tips for effective and satisfactory use of grading adaptations based on prioritization of content and related assignments. Following are the most frequently noted examples.

• Compared to other types of grading adaptations, prioritization appears to involve a great deal more time and effort, and is therefore passed over by some teachers. Teachers often rate prioritization as having many potential benefits, yet focus their discussions on other types of adaptations first. The perceived time and effort required to

Tool 6-2
Prioritizing Content in Your Scope and Sequence Chart for a Marking Period

Ranked Content	Criteria for Grading	Areas of Expectation
1.	– national standards - state standards - local standards - prerequisite for next class - important to individual student	- classwork - homework - group work - test/quiz - project
2.	– national standards - state standards - local standards - prerequisite for next class - important to individual student	- classwork - homework - group work - test/quiz - project
3.	– national standards - state standards - local standards - prerequisite for next class - important to individual student	- classwork - homework - group work - test/quiz - project
4.	– national standards - state standards - local standards - prerequisite for next class - important to individual student	- classwork - homework - group work - test/quiz - project
5.	– national standards - state standards - local standards - prerequisite for next class - important to individual student	- classwork - homework - group work - test/quiz - project
6.	– national standards - state standards - local standards - prerequisite for next class - important to individual student	- classwork - homework - group work - test/quiz - project

prioritize content and assignments, and the teacher's lack of familiarity with this process, no doubt weigh against the benefits of the adaptation. Teachers have improved the ratio of effort to benefit by using the prioritized content and related assignments for multiple students, and by identifying only the most important assignments rather than rank-ordering everything to be covered in the class.

- Teachers find prioritization to be easier and more helpful if completed before the school year begins, during the planning process for the year. Once the scope and sequence for the content and the syllabus for the class have been constructed, prioritization seems to take more time because it involves changing existing plans. Teachers should become familiar with prioritization in the spring of the school year, with the goal of prioritizing their content and assignments for the following fall. With such a head start, teachers can more easily incorporate prioritized content into the grading plan for an individual student.

Table 9 presents an implementation guide for adaptations that involve prioritization of content and related assignments. Note that the

step in which student performance is translated into grades does not necessarily involve any special procedures. That is, you may choose to apply the same grading criteria, scale, and weights to the prioritized content and related assignments as you used prior to prioritizing what you will cover in class. Or, you may choose to use additional grading adaptations in addition to prioritization.

Evaluation of Prioritization as a Grading Adaptation

Table 10 presents our evaluation matrix originally introduced in Chapter 5, now completed for grading adaptations based on prioritization. Assuming that you have prioritized your content based on recognized learning standards for all learners, this adaptation may result in grades that accurately reflect progress on the general education curriculum (#1), and result in collaboration between the special and general educators (#8). While achievement of these potential beneficial characteristics is dependent on how the adaptation is implemented, they are available for most teams. Adaptations based on prioritization may be perceived as relatively more fair by peers (#9) and other teachers (#10), although there is no research evidence to support this notion at this time. Such a hypothesis is based on the finding that teachers often prioritize content for an entire

Table 9
Implementation Guide for Adaptations Involving Prioritization of Content and Related Assignments

Adaptation	Preparing for Grading	Translating into Grades
<u>Report Card</u> Base all or most of the grade on how well the student performed on prioritized content and related assignments.	1. Identify criteria for prioritizing content. 2. Prioritize content for a short or extended period. 3. Establish grading criteria for prioritized assignments.	Apply existing grading criteria, scale and weights to prioritized content, or implement an additional grading adaptation.

class. Thus, doing so to a greater degree for an individual student may not seem so different to peers and colleagues. Most of the remaining benefits are possible if the team focuses on collaboration during the process of clarifying and implementing the adaptation. The team would have to pay special attention to how the adaptations are developed and used if they wish to achieve benefits related to student effort and motivation (#2, #4) or incorporation of progress on IEP objectives (#3).

Chapter Summary

This chapter described specific procedures for implementing a grading adaptation that involves prioritization of content and related assignments. Procedures for prioritization are different from those for other adaptations in that the actual adaptation occurs before instruction occurs, or before assignments are made. Hence, prioritization is a proactive adaptation that can be combined with other adaptations if necessary. Prioritization focuses specifically on the content, and therefore presents the potential for increased focus on the general education curriculum.

Table 10

Grading Adaptations Evaluation Matrix: Grading Adaptations Involving Prioritizing of Content and Related Assignments

Characteristic	Probable	Possible	Requires Special Attention	Comment
Effect on the Grade				
1. Produces grades that accurately reflect progress on general education curriculum.	X			1. Depends on criteria used for prioritization.
2. Produces grades that accurately reflect student effort and motivation.			X	2. May require additional adaptation.
3. Produces grades that accurately reflect progress on individual or IEP learning goals.		X		3. May require additional adaptation.
4. Produces grades that will motivate student to try hard in the future.	X		X	4. May require additional adaptation.
Effect on Grading Process				
5. Results in collaboration between teachers and parents.			X	5. If parents are invited to participate in the prioritization process.
6. Results in collaboration between special and general educators.	X			6. Teachers should work together on prioritization.
7. Results in coordination of the classroom accommodations and how the student is graded.		X		7. Accommodations could be defined after prioritized content has been identified.
8. Results in access to the general education curriculum.	X			8. Depends on criteria used for prioritization.
Effect on Community Perspectives				
9. Perceived as fair by typical classmates.		X		9. May depend on awareness that teachers use prioritization for entire class. Otherwise could look as if some students were required to do less.
10. Perceived as fair by other teachers.		X		10. Same issue as for students.

Suggested Activities

The following activities are suggested for getting started on implementing grading adaptations involving prioritization:

- Review the various criteria or standards you might use to prioritize your content for students with disabilities. Gather available information on learning standards, your school curriculum, and course descriptions for advanced courses in your content area. Look for areas of agreement between the different sources. Discuss strategies for prioritizing with your colleagues.

- Start small by prioritizing just the content in one unit or chapter for your class. Consider whether prioritizing might actually help in organizing your lessons.

- Consider talking with your students and their parents about how to decide what is most important for the student to learn. Don't expect them to have knowledge of the content in your class, but do listen for them to say, for example, that they want the student to know things that will help him in more difficult classes, in college, or in the workplace. Take time to explain to them why your state or school has learning standards.

Where Do We Go From Here?

This chapter is the first of five that will describe specific procedures for implementing grading adaptations. The next chapter proceeds to look at adaptations that involve balancing the components of a grading system. Specifically, the next chapter will describe how to consider products, processes and effort in your grading system.

CHAPTER 7
Adjusting the Components of a Balanced Grading System

This chapter will describe the following procedures for implementing grading adaptations that involve components of a balanced grading system:

- Identifying sources and opportunities for students to demonstrate processes or effort

- Determining when or how increasing emphasis on use of processes or expenditure of effort will benefit the student

- Establishing an effective balance between product, process, and effort in your grading system

Chapter 4 described the relationship between products, processes, and effort in a balanced grading system. It was discussed then that most grading systems emphasize the quality of student products, often excluding consideration of processes or effort. Or, when effort is considered it is done so haphazardly. Given the wide-spread lack of familiarity with grading process use and effort, this chapter is dedicated to those two components of the balanced grading process.

Measuring a Student's Use of Processes

When considering incorporating process use into a grading system for an entire class or an individual student with a disability, we must be able to answer the following questions: (a) what processes do my students (or does my student) need to use to be successful on the work I assign? and (b) which of the processes that students can or should use can be incorporated into my grading system?

Procedures for answering these questions will be described in the following sections. However, it must first be said, in our research, we have observed that teams have derived significant benefit from pursuing the above questions, regardless of whether or not they eventually chose to implement a grading adaptation that considers use of processes. It seems that special educators are more sensitized to process use because (a) they studied processes such as learning strategies in their preservice coursework, and (b) they have worked individually with students and have observed students attempting to use tools or strategies. When the special and general educators collaborate to complete the procedures to be described, true sharing of expertise occurs.

What Processes Does My Student Need to Use to Be Successful on Assignments?

Following are two procedures for pinpointing processes a student could or should use: (a) a task analysis of individual assignments, and (b) identifying processes described in the student's IEP. We will describe each separately.

Analyzing Assignments

Remember that we are using the term "processes" here to describe both covert (e.g., self-instruction, self-talk) and overt (e.g., complete a checklist) actions a student takes to complete a task or assignment. These covert and overt actions are often referred to as "learning strategies," a major topic of research and practice in the past 20 years (e.g., Deshler, Ellis, & Lenz, 1996). This book does not lend itself to a thorough discussion of learning strategies and strategy use. However, general and special educators with knowledge of strategies will be particularly effective in serving their students with disabilities, especially students in the middle/secondary grades.

The IDEA (1997) requires that assistive technology be considered for all students at the time that their (IEP) is developed or reviewed (Bateman & Linden, 2001). At this point, awareness of the types of technology that may be helpful for students with disabilities is still growing (Hasselbring, 2001).

Teams are urged to review their knowledge of assistive technologies before determining whether a grading adaptation involving technology is an option for a particular student. One tool the author has found particularly helpful in facilitating assistive technology consideration is a technology integration framework (Edyburn, 2002) shown in Table 11. While the purpose of this book is not to promote the use of assistive technology, such an emphasis is now present in the legal guidelines and the use of technology is a fast-growing process that more and more stu-

Table 11
Examples of Technology to Support IEP Goals

The purpose of this section is to highlight common instructional challenges and how selected products can be used to address the difficulties of students with disabilities and others who struggle to be successful academically. Listings are illustrative and not comprehensive. No endorsement is implied. Explore the possibilities.

Instructional Challenge	Strategy	Technology Possibilities
Difficulty remembering appointments, things to do, reminders, etc.	Provide a reminder service that calls the person with a reminder.	Mr. WakeUp http://www.iping.com
	Provide web-based calendar and personal planner.	My Yahoo! http://my.yahoo.com DayRunner http://www.dayrunner.com Franklin Covey http://www.franklincovey.com
	Provide a personal digital assistant.	PalmPilot http://www.palm.com PDA Page http://www.pdapage.com
Difficulty remembering factual information.	Teach the individual how to use online ready reference tools.	Ask Jeeves for Kids http://www.ajkids.com Ask Jeeves http://www.askjeeves.com
Inability to complete homework.	Provide instruction on study skills.	Center for Electronic Studying http://ces.uoregon.edu/ The Study Skills Strategies Home Page http://www.d.uwm.edu/student/loon/acad/strat/ Study Guides and Strategies http://www.iss.stthomas.edu/studyguides/
	Create interactive learning activities as an alternative to completing paper and pencil assignments.	QuizStar http://quiz.4teachers.org QuizCenter http://school.discovery.com/quizcenter/quizcenter.html

Table 11 continued

Instructional Challenge	Strategy	Technology Possibilities

Inability to read at grade level.	Text-to-speech software allows a student to listen to printed material that s/he cannot read independently.	CAST eReader
		    http://www.cast.org/
		ReadPlease
		    http://www.readplease.com
		Write Out:Loud
		    http://www.donjohnston.con
		WordQ
		    http://www.wordq.com

	Access texts (i.e., literature) that are in the public domain for use with text-to-speech software.	InfoMotions
		    http://www.infomotions.com
		Project Gutenberg
		    http://promo.net/pg/

	Provide a hand-held scanner that the individual can use to scan unknown words.	The Reading Pen http://www.wizcomtech.com

	Use specially designed instructional materials that are written at multiple reading levels.	Start-to-Finish Books
		    http://www.donjohnston.con
		Windows on the Universe
		    http://www.windows.ucar.ec

Difficulties in reading that limit awareness of current events.	Provide alternative formats for accessing current events information.	News-2-You
		    http://www.news-2-you.com
		My Yahoo!
		    http://my.yahoo.com
		EarthWeek
		    http://www.earthweek.com

Difficulties in generating ideas for writing.	Use a brainstorming tool to generate ideas and begin organizing the writing project.	Kidspiration
		    http://www.inspiration.com
		Inspiration
		    http://www.inspiration.com
		Draft Builder
		    http://www.donjohnston.

Adpated and updated from: Edyburn, D. L. (2002). Technology integratio resource guide. *Special Education Technology Practice, 4*(1), 20-26. Reprinted wit permission of Knowledge by Design, Inc.

dents will be required to use in the future. Thus, technology use is a fertile area for grading adaptations that involves grading of process use. For example, students with disabilities that affect their reading decoding and comprehension may be taught strategies (e.g., looking for context clues) to compensate for their disability. Current technology might allow this student to listen to the text while reading it on the computer screen, and click on unknown words to access a thesaurus that gives a definition. When teams provide assistive technology to students, they expect them to learn to use the device and to use it regularly. Therefore, the technology should be considered a type of process that the student must use, not simply an accommodation. If teams consider efficient use of assistive technology as a process, they can logically consider assigning part of a student's grade to performance with the technology.

Returning to the topic of analyzing your assignment, readers are referred to Tool 7-1, designed to guide you in analyzing an individual assignment for processes. The example of Tool 7-1 presented here has been completed for a language arts assignment – writing a five paragraph essay. In the far-left column you list the steps a student must follow to complete the assignment. If you have never completed a task analysis before, you may be unaccustomed to "dissecting" your assignments to this degree. A general rule of thumb is to consider every step your student must complete in order to access (e.g., read, listen, open) information, organize work, and create a product. It is important not to bypass a step (e.g., take notes) just because most of your students can do it effortlessly.

Let's review Tool 7-1 as it has been completed for an assignment in a language arts class. In the first column (left), the teacher(s) has listed the steps in the assignment. They identified the steps by considering how the assignment will be explained to the class. In the second column, the teachers indicated how they thought most students would complete each of the steps. Note that the content of this column may vary across classrooms because teachers may teach their students to follow different steps to complete an assignment. In fact, the processes prescribed for an entire class may include one or several that are especially helpful to a student with a disability. For example, the teachers completing Tool 7-1 have included graphic organizers, teacher-provided format, editing checklist, and word processing as processes for all students to use. All of these processes have been identified as advantageous for students with disabilities as well.

Tool 7-1
Analyzing Processes in Assignments

> Students with disabilities may have difficulty with processes that most typical students complete effortlessly. Also, students with disabilities may have to learn to use different processes that help them overcome the effects of their disability. It is important that general and special educators collaborate to identify the processes embedded in an assignment, and to pinpoint processes that a student with a disability may need to use in order to complete the assignment.

Example: Five-Paragraph Essay

Steps to Complete Assignment	Processes Most Students Use	What an Individual Student Needs to Do	Related IEP Objective	Type of Process
1. Brainstorm a topic	Dialogue with a peer or teacher	Develop timeline for entire assignment		___ learning strategy ___ assistive technology _X_ self-management strategy
2. Create a graphic organizer using the topic	Work with teacher to identify important components of topic on graphic organizer supplied by the teacher	Electronic speller / dictionary / thesaurus		___ learning strategy ___ assistive technology _X_ self-management strategy
3. Outline five paragraphs	Follow format provided by the teacher			___ learning strategy ___ assistive technology _X_ self-management strategy

Tool 7-1 continued

Steps to Complete Assignment	Processes Most Students Use	What an Individual Student Needs to Do	Related IEP Objective	Type of Process
4. Write rough draft	Use outline and word processor to write rough draft	Use word processor with word prediction		___ learning strategy _X_ assistive technology ___ self-management strategy
5. Edit rough draft	Use editing checklist provided by the teacher. Submit product for peer review			___ learning strategy ___ assistive technology _X_ self-management strategy
6. Write final draft (publish)	Make necessary changes using the word processor			___ learning strategy ___ assistive technology _X_ self-management strategy

Had the teachers not emphasized such processes for the entire class, they may have listed them in the third category dedicated to processes that a particular student could or should use to complete the assignment. Two additional processes have been identified for this particular student to use. The first is an electronic speller that the student uses to check spelling when not using a word processor, or when the student needs to check the definition of a word. The second process involves a personal timeline that the student will develop and monitor. The timeline includes each of the steps in the assignment, the date they are due, and a space for his parents and teacher to verify completion of a step.

In the fourth column the teachers check the types of processes the student could or should use to complete an assignment. We encourage checking processes that are expected for all students because the team may decide to place additional emphasis on the process by incorporating it into the grading process for a particular student in the class. The final column prompts the team to refer to any of the student's IEP objectives that may be related to strategy use. We will discuss the significance of IEP objectives related to processes next.

Processes Described in the IEP

Processes for students to use in completing their classwork are found in the IEP in an obvious place, such as the learning objectives, and in a less obvious place, such as the list of accommodations being made for the student. Process use, in turn, is indicated in IEP objectives that require the student to use strategies to enhance their reading, writing, or mathematical performances. Too often, objectives do not specify the precise type of strategy a student is to use, nor do they indicate that the student should generate a strategy, although this has been shown to be as or more effective than teacher generated strategies for some students. The top portion of Table 12 presents examples of IEP objectives, some of which we have observed, that refer to strategy use.

While you probably expected that IEP objectives would address strategy use, you may not have considered that students must employ processes in order to use several types of accommodations that we provide in the classroom. Teachers find it helpful to categorize accommodations based on whether they "balance expectations" or "build new skills."

Accommodations that balance expectations are those that reduce or

Table 12
Processes Embedded in the IEP

Examples of IEP Objectives	Type of Process
Tom will use a strategy to correctly solve math word problems.	_X_ learning strategy ___ assistive technology ___ self-management
Sally will use all functions in a word processing program to produce a three page essay with 0-1 errors in spelling, grammar or punctuation.	___ learning strategy _X_ assistive technology ___ self-management
Todd will write his assignments in his homework log and have his parents check completed work nightly for one month.	___ learning strategy ___ assistive technology _X_ self-management
Examples of Accommodations	**Type of Process**
Provide audiotape version of science textbook.	___ learning strategy _X_ assistive technology ___ self-management
Allow student to revise papers and resubmit for additional points.	_X_ learning strategy ___ assistive technology ___ self-management
Provide assistance with homework during 7th hour support period.	___ learning strategy ___ assistive technology _X_ self-management

eliminate a barrier to student success caused by the student's disability. Examples of such accommodations include special reading materials and instructions to low readers, modifying assignments to make them shorter and allowing students to dictate responses to test questions rather than write the answers. Without accom- modations that balance expectations, many students with disabilities could not meet even minimal expectations in the general education classroom. Such adaptations reduce the demand on the student to improve skills in the area impacted most by presence of a disability.

Another type of accommodation also appears in student's IEPs. Accommodations that involve the student using a special tool or technology to complete his work require that the student learn to use the accommodation effectively and consistently. Such accommodations actively "build new skills," rather than just balancing expectations.

As stated earlier, the general and special educator may have different knowledge and experience with processes and with the content of an IEP. Therefore, both teachers are encouraged to collaborate in completing Tool 7-2 for identifying processes in the student's IEP.

Measuring and Grading Student Effort

Incorporating a measure of student effort into a classroom or individualized grading system requires that you can: (a) pinpoint how and when a student's effort warrants special emphasis, and (b) establish an objective means of measuring and reporting effort. No guidelines exist for determining when a student will benefit from more emphasis on effort in the grading system.

It is logical to assume that measuring and grading effort will serve as a means of rewarding and motivating students who must exert sig-

nificant effort to complete their work in general education classrooms. This is often a student who struggles in reading and writing, and who must spend much more time than classmates to complete even routine assignments. Often, such a student has to complete more work at home than nondisabled peers. Obviously, such a student should be encouraged to continue to work hard and basing part of the student's grade on effort may be an effective strategy toward that end.

But does giving a grade for effort have a downside? Perhaps, if we consider that the relationship between effort and achievement is not always predictable, a student may work hard but still master little of the content for the class. Your team should answer these questions when considering incorporating effort into your grading system:

- Does the team have evidence that when the student tries harder, the student performs better on assignments?

- Can the team agree on how to measure effort?

- Will the student perceive the adaptation as an incentive to keep working hard?

Tool 7-2
Evaluating Processes to Be Incorporated into the Grading Process

Processes	Criteria
List the processes you found when analyzing an assignment.	
1.	- very important for completing work in this class - very important for completing future work - grading process may motivate student - very important for increasing student independence
2.	- very important for completing work in this class - very important for completing future work - grading process may motivate student - very important for increasing student independence
3.	- very important for completing work in this class - very important for completing future work - grading process may motivate student - very important for increasing student independence
4.	- very important for completing work in this class - very important for completing future work - grading process may motivate student - very important for increasing student independence
List the processes that are described in the student's IEP objectives	
1.	- very important for completing work in this class - very important for completing future work - grading process may motivate student - very important for increasing student independence
2.	- very important for completing work in this class - very important for completing future work - grading process may motivate student - very important for increasing student independence
3.	- very important for completing work in this class - very important for completing future work - grading process may motivate student - very important for increasing student independence

Tool 7-2 continued

Processes	Criteria
List the process that the student must use to take advantage of accommodations	
1.	- very important for completing work in this class - very important for completing future work - grading process may motivate student - very important for increasing student independence
2.	- very important for completing work in this class - very important for completing future work - grading process may motivate student - very important for increasing student independence
3.	- very important for completing work in this class - very important for completing future work - grading process may motivate student - very important for increasing student independence
4.	- very important for completing work in this class - very important for completing future work - grading process may motivate student - very important for increasing student independence
5.	- very important for completing work in this class - very important for completing future work - grading process may motivate student - very important for increasing student independence
6.	- very important for completing work in this class - very important for completing future work - grading process may motivate student - very important for increasing student independence

Table 13
Student Behaviors Representing Effort and Dimensions for Measuring Them

Student Behaviors	Dimensions for Measurement
Completing math problems	- Number of problems completed
Reading	- Words read - Pages read - Pages summarized
Writing	- Number of words, sentences, or paragraphs written - Number of errors corrected
Completing homework	- Number of days to complete assignments - Number or percentage of assignments completed
Asking questions	- Number of topic-related questions asked - Number of clarification questions asked same day as assignment - Number of times student raised hand
Using supports	- Number of times assistance sought from teacher - Percentage of assignments in which student seeks help for difficult parts - Percentage of days student uses study period to get help with homework that day

If your team answers no to any of the above questions, you may want to reconsider the idea of grading the student's effort.

Teams that do wish to pursue a grading adaptation should begin by determining how effort will be measured. Table 13 presents examples of student behaviors that may constitute effort, along with suggested dimensions for measuring such behaviors. Once your team has identified a specific behavior(s) that you wish to measure, you will need to determine how to incorporate effort into the grading system.

Tips from Teachers

Teachers participating in our research projects have reported or demonstrated several insights and experiences related to implementing grading adaptations involving a balanced grading process. Following are several of the more common tips.

- Respect the fact that the types of processes that are described in this chapter are relatively new to many teachers and were not thoroughly covered in their preservice programs or in professional development activities. This is especially true for assistive technologies, which is still an emerging field for many districts and teachers.

- To avoid defensiveness or embarrassment, teachers should discuss privately the processes their students can or do use before talking with parents. General educators often look to the special educator for expertise in learning strategies, assistive technology and self-management. However, this expectation may not be accurate or fair, as the knowledge and expertise of special educators varies depending on their training and previous teaching experiences. To minimize resistance, approach the area of process use as a learning opportunity for all team members, with an expectation that both teachers will be able to learn more from readings or consultations with colleagues.

- Grading students on process use

does not require extensive expertise in learning strategies, assistive technology, or self management strategies. It does require a willingness to analyze assignments and review sources of information that are readily available to all teachers.

- Consider whether the processes you wish the student with an IEP to use would also be helpful for other students in the class, or whether they are already being used by some students. For example, strategies for planning and editing written work may be beneficial to many students, and can therefore be integrated into the instruction for the entire class. Teachers have reported that while contemplating processes for a particular student, they were able to identify processes for which they should be providing instruction during the lesson. As they have related, teams tend to overlook strategy use when most of the class can do it covertly, automatically, and without help from the teacher.

- Teachers seem to approach grading effort in two ways. One approach is to increase the value of effort because the student is already working hard and the teachers wish to reward the effort. The other is to acknowledge that the student will not be able to earn a higher grade based on any performance other than effort; therefore, it is fair to increase the value of effort. This approach is similar to changing the grading scale or weights in that the student's performance can remain constant but the grade will rise. An alternative approach is to increase the value of effort as a means for motivating the student to try harder. For students with disabilities, the relationship between effort and grades on their products may not be clear, or they may have experienced no relationship. Therefore, when they are encouraged to study harder, turn in more homework, or ask more questions in class, they may not perceive the value of such efforts. By adding points or value for the effort, teams allow the student to experience immediate benefits to effort. And in most cases, increased effort will produce additional benefits such as improved performances on test/quizzes because the student is better prepared for all assignments.

In the author's experience, most parents and teachers prefer the second approach to grading effort because it involves a positive and naturally occurring consequence for the student's effort, and suggests that the student may have the abilities to improve overall performance if the student expends the effort. The earlier approach can be viewed as acknowledging that the student's performance cannot improve, and therefore we should shift attention to effort so that the student can earn a higher grade. While logical and probably appropriate for some students with more severe disabilities, this approach should be used prudently.

Implementing Adaptations That Involve Process and Effort

Table 14 depicts the implementation guide completed for adaptations that involve incorporating process use and effort. Note that a major step in translating performance with processes or effort into a grade involves deciding whether multiple grades will be given for assignments. As stated in Chapter 5, giving multiple grades that include a grade for process use and/or effort is perceived as relatively more helpful by teachers, and as fairer by students without disabilities. Assigning multiple grades also allows you to grade the actual product the student produced, thus avoiding the dilemma of rewarding process use when the student still produces an incomplete or low quality product.

Table 14

Implementation Guide for Adaptations Involving Process Use and Effort

Adaptation	Preparing for Grading	Translating into Grades
Daily Work		
Base all or part of the grade for an assignment on processes used by the student to complete work.	1. Identify processes to be measured. 2. Identify criteria for grading use of process.	1. Determine if process use is part of grade or multiple grade. 2. Convert percent accuracy into a grade. 3. Combine grade with grade for product or effort, or record as multiple grade and average in for report card grade.
Base all or part of the grade for an assignment on student's performance with supports that "build new skills."	1. Identify processes to be measured. 2. Identify criteria for grading use of process.	1. Determine if process use is part of grade or multiple grade. 2. Convert percent accuracy into a grade. 3. Combine grade with grade for product or effort, or record as multiple grade and average in for report card grade.
Base part of the grade for an assignment on the student's effort.	Identify how effort will be defined and measured.	Same as for process use grade.
Report Card Grades		
Base part of the grade on an overall measure of effort for the marking period.	1. Identify how overall effort will be defined 2. Design system for measuring effort accurately throughout the marking period.	Incorporate effort as an expectation area in your grading system and assign a specified weight (e.g., 10%) toward the report card grade.

Evaluation of Grading Adaptations that Involve Processes and Effort

Table 15 presents the evaluation matrix completed for adaptations involving process use and effort. This type of grading adaptation has good potential for producing grades that accurately reflect student effort and motivation (#2), accurately reflect progress on individual IEP learning objectives (#3), and motivate the student to try harder (#4). The extent to which the adaptation reflects progress on the IEP objectives depends on whether or not the student is graded on processes identified with Tool 7-2. The extent to which the adaptation produces product grades that accurately reflect progress on the general education curriculum (#1) will depend on the balance that is maintained between the product, process, and effort grades. For example, if too much weight is given to effort, the student's grade may be higher than would be expected based on the quality of the work completed. Hence, a careful balance must be determined with input from the entire team.

Adaptations that involve process use and effort are likely to produce collaboration between teachers (#6), and with parents if they are invited to provide input (#5). It is hard to imagine an adaptation involving measuring process use and effort that is not designed and monitored together by the special and general educator. Given that student effort and process use are often evidenced in performance on homework, parental input and monitoring also seems necessary and logical. Grading adaptations involving process use and effort should result in coordination with classroom accommodations (#7) because of the need for teachers to distinguish when processes are being used to balance expectations versus when they are being used to build new skills. If students are expected to learn to use a new strategy or assistive technology device, the teachers should provide instruction on how to use the processes and then fade support until the student is able to complete the process independently. Grading adaptations that involve process use or effort should reflect the level of support provided.

Regarding the perceived fairness of the adaptations, several factors require consideration. We reported in Chapter 4 that basing part of a student's grade on process use was perceived as helpful by general education teachers, while students perceived basing part of a grade on effort as being more fair than several other types of adaptations. Here, it may be necessary to consider process use and effort separately.

Table 15
Grading Adaptations Evaluation Matrix: Adaptations Involving Process Use and Effort

Characteristic	Probable	Possible	Requires Special Attention	Comment
Effect on the Grade				
1. Produces grades that accurately reflect progress on general education curriculum.		X		1. Depends on balance of product, process and effort.
2. Produces grades that accurately reflect student effort and motivation.	X			2. Assuming that effort is measured.
3. Produces grades that accurately reflect progress on individual or IEP learning goals.	X			3. Assuming that processes are identified in IEP with Tool 7-?
4. Produces grades that will motivate student to try hard in the future.	X			4. Assuming that student has input on how effort and process will be measured.
Effect on Grading Process				
5. Results in collaboration between teachers and parents.		X		5. Depends on parents being invited to provide input.
6. Results in collaboration between special and general educators.	X			6. Assuming both teachers have input into how process use and effort will be defined and measured.
7. Results in coordination of the classroom accommodations and how the student is graded.		X		7. Teachers should distinguish between supports for building skills vs. balancing expectations
8. Results in access to the general education curriculum.		X		8. If processes and effort are measured with general education curriculum.
Effect on Community Perspectives				
9. Perceived as fair by typical classmates.		X		9. May depend on awareness process use by all students, and balance of product, process and effort in overall grading system
10. Perceived as fair by other teachers.		X		10. May depend on extent to which process use and effort improve performance on overall quality of products.

Regarding grading process use, perceived fairness may be influenced by the teacher's use of the practice for the whole class on some assignments. Also, the extent to which improving process use will have a direct impact on the overall quality of the student's work may influence perceptions of other teachers. For example, basing part of a student's grade on effective use of text-to-speech software may seem more fair if the observer can clearly identify how the software improves the student's performance on writing assignments.

Perceptions regarding the grading of effort may hinge on the balance that is maintained in the grading process. Although grading on effort may seem relatively more fair for students with disabilities, students and teachers still expect that all students are graded in part on the quality of their work. Thus, an A earned on an incomplete or poorly written assignment will likely cause concern, regardless of the effort the student put forth. As stated earlier in this chapter, teams should attempt to measure effort that also results in improved overall performance in the classroom.

Chapter Summary

This chapter has described specific procedures for implementing grading adaptations that involve adjusting the balance of products, processes, and effort in your grading system. Rather than treat adaptations for effort and processes individually, they are presented along with a description of products to emphasize that grading systems for all students often consider products, processes, and effort, and that an adaptation is made only when the balance between the three is adjusted to meet the needs of a particular student.

Adaptations that involve grading effort or process use are among the more commonly used adaptations. Perhaps processes will be considered in more grading systems when teachers gain more knowledge of how students can use learning or metacognitive strategies, assistive technologies, or self-management strategies to complete their work in the general education classroom. As accountability for students with disabilities increases, strategies or technologies that allow them to access more of the general education curriculum, perhaps more independently, will likely gain in popularity. As educators become more familar with these types of processes that students use, related grading adaptations may also become more appealing.

Suggested Activities

The following activities are suggested for getting started on grading adaptations involving adjusting the balance of product, process and effort in your grading system.

- Initiate a discussion about how your colleagues balance products, processes, and effort in their current grading systems. It may be helpful to explain what is meant by "processes," as some teachers may not be familiar with the term. Point out how different balances are struck by different teachers. Discuss when and why teachers have adjusted the balance between products, processes, and effort in their grading systems.

- Gain more knowledge about learning strategies, assistive technologies, or self management strategies by talking with experienced colleagues or by reading professional literature on these topics. Journals such as *Teaching Exceptional Children* or *Intervention in School and Clinic* present practitioner oriented articles on processes that students can use to be successful.

- Start small by pointing out one strategy your students should use to complete their work and evaluating their use of the strategy as part of their grade for an assignment. You might also consider asking your students what processes they use as a first step.

- Find out if your district has a coordinator or leader for assistive technology. If so, schedule time to discuss the types of assistive technologies that are available to your students. Don't assume that you will be introduced to technologies that might be helpful for your students. Rather, seek out colleagues with expertise and begin to identify devices your students could use for reading, writing, or mathematics.

Where Do We Go From Here?

In the last two chapters you have become familiar with specific procedures for implementing grading adaptations that involve prioritizing content and balancing your grading system. These adaptations are often used informally by teachers, and are relevant for most students.

The next chapter will describe procedures for implementing the only grading adaptation for students with disabilities only–grading progress on IEP objectives.

CHAPTER 8
Measuring and Grading
Progress on IEP Objectives

This chapter will describe the following procedures for implementing grading adaptations that involve progress on IEP objectives:

- Identifying existing IEP objectives that are or could be addressed through instruction in the general education classroom.

- Determining when the student may benefit from a grading system that incorporates progress on objectives.

- Determine how to measure and translate progress into a grade.

Chapter 4 presented a rationale for incorporating progress on objectives into the grading system for an individual student. Teachers who have participated in our research have told us that even a discussion regarding this adaptation, regardless of whether the adaptation is implemented, is informative.

Often, the general educator is only vaguely familiar with the specific content of the IEPs for students in their classes. Thus, it is easy to understand why consideration is seldom given to addressing IEP objectives in general education instruction, let alone incorporating progress on these objectives into the grade for the class. A prerequisite to using progress for grading is that the team perceives the IEP to be a valid description of the student's strengths and needs, and that the annual goals and objectives accurately reflect the student's present performance and needs. When IEP objectives are viewed as outdated, inaccurate, or irrelevant, the team will not perceive any potential benefit to grading progress. Indeed, we have noted that discussions regarding grading progress on IEP objectives sometimes produces honest and objective opinions regarding the perceived validity of the IEP.

This chapter will describe how to use existing IEP objectives for grading purposes. Readers are encouraged to consider revising a student's IEP if you find that the current objectives do not seem valid, or if the team wishes to increase opportunities to address IEP objectives in the general education classroom.

Identifying IEP Objectives

To reiterate, a decision to incorporate progress on objectives into a grading system may be based on: (a) the degree to which the student's progress on the objective will directly affect performance on the classroom curriculum; (b) the degree to which progress on the objective will allow the student to function more independently in the classroom and curriculum; and (c) the amount of emphasis, time, and effort placed on the objective by the student's team. In other words, the student's performance on the objective should be so important as to be considered part of the student's instruction in the class.

Tool 8-1 is designed to guide the team in evaluating potential objectives for grading. In addition to the three criteria described earlier, two additional criteria have been included regarding access to the general education classroom and feasibility of the student having ample opportunities to work on the objective in the general education classroom.

No guidelines for identifying objectives for grading have been re-

ported in the professional literature, and our own research has not investigated this specific topic. However, teachers or teams can interpret their responses to Tool 8-1 in meaningful ways that will inform their use of this type of grading adaptation. For example, an objective that requires Nicole to "read a 4 to 6 paragraph section from a 4th-grade level text and answer literal questions regarding the main characters, action, and summary" may be evaluated by her team for possible incorporation into the grading system. Because the objective focuses on comprehension of narrative or prose texts, it may not be feasible for Nicole to work on the skill regularly in science, health, or social studies because those classes presumably rely on expository texts. Furthermore, her progress on the objective may not be expected to generalize to comprehension of expository texts. Therefore, teachers in those content area courses could not mark any of the boxes on the evaluation form. However, the language arts teacher may use novels and essays as materials for the class. Additionally, the class activities and assignments may all involve reading, comprehending, and interpreting texts, which would mean ample opportunity for Nicole to work on this skill. In all likelihood, the language arts teacher would mark all of the boxes in Tool 8-1, and may therefore seriously consider incorpo-

Tool 8-1
Evaluating IEP Objectives for Grading on Progress Adaptation

IEP Objectives	How will progress directly affect performance in class curriculum?	How will progress increase independent functioning?	Is significant emphasis placed on work addressing this objective?	How will progress increase access to general education curriculum?	Can objective be addressed regularly in general education class?	Comments
1.						
2.						
3.						
4.						
5.						

rating progress on the objective as a grading adaptation for Nicole. If we were to substitute "expository text" for "narrative text" in the objective, each teacher would likely reverse their responses on Tool 8-1 because Nicole's improvement in comprehending expository texts could have a significant impact on her performance in all classes.

Some IEP objectives may not have clear implications for work in content area class. That is, objectives that involve written expression may be more or less relevant to a student's performance in a content area class. For example, Anthony may have an IEP objective requiring him to write a correct paragraph. His teachers in social studies, health, or science may not assign work that requires writing complete paragraphs. Or, Anthony's teachers may actually be modifying his assignments so that he can use phrases to answer questions on homework or tests. Perhaps Anthony's tests are modified to reduce writing in general. In such a case, the team must determine if Anthony should be encouraged to write paragraphs in a content area class before even considering a grading adaptation that includes progress on the objective. As teams become more familiar with grading adaptations, their perspectives on whom to use bypass accommodations with versus building skills

through IEP objectives may be influenced. That is, momentum for working to build skills through IEP objectives may be stronger if the student's progress can be incorporated into the grading system. The student and his parents may be more motivated to pursue skill building, even if challenging, if progress can be captured by the grading system.

Measuring Progress

To accurately grade a student's progress, we must first have a measurable behavior and a dimension in which to measure the behavior. For example, an objective for improving written expression should indicate that the student will "write" a specified number of words, sentences, or paragraphs. We can measure writing by counting the words, sentences, paragraphs. Once you have determined that an IEP objective does indeed include a measurable behavior, you may benefit from using Tool 8-2, which is designed to guide you through the steps for determining how to measure progress on an objective.

The second column in Tool 8-2 contains a checklist of dimensions commonly used to measure student performances. The dimensions of accuracy, rate, and frequency are self-explanatory. "Level of support" refers to the level of teacher support

Tool 8-2
Preparing IEP Objectives for Grading

IEP Objective	Dimension for Measuring	How Progress Will be Measured	How Progress Will Be Monitored	How Progress Will Be Translated to Grade	Incorporating into Grade
	- accuracy - rate - frequency - level of support - rubric score - other (specify)	- percentages for accuracy - rate - level of independence - total frequency - met/unmet - rubric score - other (specify)	__ same assignments as rest of class __ special probes given on a schedule to the student __ assignments modified to provide work on the objective	- convert percentages to grades - convert total frequences to grade - convert mean rate to grade - convert met/unmet to grade - convert total rubric scores - other (specify)	- separate grade - multiple grade - part of grade in other area

required for a student to perform the skill described in the objective. The ultimate criterion is usually that the student will perform the skill independently, with no supports. When level of support is the dimension to be measured, you need to clarify all of the teacher supports (e.g., prompts, cues) that may be given so that everyone on the team is clear on what "independent" means. The dimension "rubric score" denotes a score or point total a student receives on a performance that is assessed with a rubric. Rubrics are designed to provide a holistic score that includes evaluation of several different performance areas. For example, a rubric for evaluating a student essay may include separate scores for originality, clarity, and correct use of conventions (e.g., spelling).

The third column describes ways in which dimensions can be summarized to measure progress. Possible methods include calculating percentages for overall accuracy, calculating a mean, median, a final rate, declaring the objective as met or unmet, or calculating a summative score on a rubric. Determining how progress will be calculated or reported is a critical step in establishing the validity of the grading adaptation. Note that the decision to express progress as the objective being "met" or "unmet" will make it difficult to convert progress to a grade. For example, does "met" translate into a passing grade of D, or the highest grade of A?

The fourth column contains the information that may be most critical to implementing IEP objectives in the general education classroom – how the student's performance will be assessed. Indeed, teachers who have participated in our projects and workshops have lamented that IEP objectives are often not written in terms that suggest a way to measure student progress in the general education classroom. In column four we describe three potential ways in which a student's progress on an IEP objective might be measured in the general education classroom: (a) the same assignments completed by the rest of the class; (b) special probes or assessments designed to measure progress on a particular skill and administered to the student on a schedule; or (c) assignments based on those for the rest of the class, but modified to provide an opportunity for the student to demonstrate progress on an IEP objective. Using an IEP objective that involves improvement in reading comprehension, for example, an included student may be assessed with the same tests or projects completed by classmates, by specially designed probes that are given to the student every Friday, or by modified assignments that require the student to answer comprehension questions each time reading is assigned.

The fifth column describes how a measure of progress can be translated into a grade. The most obvious strategy is to develop a scale similar to those typically used for grading, in which total points or overall percentages are aligned with a scale of letter/number grades. For example, an objective that requires a student to read a specified number of words correctly could yield at least two measures:

total words read correctly and percentage of words read correctly. If the readings are timed, a measure of rate of words read correctly is now available. The above measures are easily converted to a grade by aligning the total number of words, or percentage of words, with a grade. Converting a summative rubric score to a grade is similar to the process for converting a total number of points, or an overall percentage, to a grade. The scale for assigning a grade to a rubric score should be determined ahead of time and communicated clearly to the student and parents.

No doubt you are anxiously awaiting suggestions for assigning grades to measures of progress. Two approaches seem logical. The first would be to align the top of the grading scale (e.g., A) with the criteria for mastery stated in the objective. For instance, if Hilda was to construct a three-paragraph essay with 0 - 2 errors, such a performance should earn an A. If Hilda approximates the mastery criterion by writing fewer than three correct paragraphs, or makes more than two errors, then she will receive a lower grade. The key in this scenario is for her teachers to have predetermined the criteria for earning grades A - F, and have communicated them clearly to Hilda and her parents.

Another method for grading progress is to align a specified amount of progress with a grade. For example, a student making a gain of 25% on an IEP objective may earn an A. This system may be best suited for grading progress on objectives that are unlikely to be met in just one or two marking periods. The key to using this strategy effectively is to develop fair and accurate intervals of progress (e.g., 15%, 50 words, 5 sentences) that will challenge the student but not make it impossible for the student to make a desirable grade.

You may be thinking that measuring progress on IEP objectives and converting progress to a grade is a time consuming endeavor. However, this grading adaptation is an important strategy for integrating a student's IEP into the general education classroom instruction and for grading a student's performance on his most important learning objectives as determined by the student's team.

Tips from Teachers

Teachers participating in our research projects have provided many insights on how or when to use grading adaptations that involve progress on objectives. Following are several of the most common.

- Make sure everyone agrees on the validity of an IEP objective before attempting to implement it and measure progress in the general education classroom. If the special or general educator seems reluctant to work out the details for grading progress, consider that the resistance stems from lack of confidence in the contents of the objectives. Teachers often report that IEP objectives were developed the prior year and may not seem appropriate for expectations being placed on the student in the general education classroom(s). Another common problem is measuring progress on an objective by assessing performance in the general education classroom. Although a tool for working through the details of measuring progress has been provided, teams may prefer to generate new objectives that better reflect what the student must do in the current classroom(s). Revising IEP objectives may seem time consuming. However, it may be more satisfying and effective than trying to make unworkable objectives workable.

- Consider whether the short term objectives in the IEP are roughly aligned with the marking periods for the year. Short term objectives are often written to be completed by the end of a marking period (typically 9 or 12 weeks). If this is the case, teachers may choose to use the criteria for the objective as the criteria for grading. When the number of objectives does not match the number of marking periods, teachers must determine the criteria for grading progress on an objective. One way is to use the criteria stated for the annual or long-term goal, but this may be too difficult for a student to achieve in just the first, second, or third marking periods. Obviously, a student should not receive a lower grade because the student made only partial progress on a goal that was written to be met at the end of the year.

Table 16 presents the implementation guide for adaptations involving progress on IEP objectives. We have discussed procedures for measuring progress and converting progress to a grade previously. Once you have measured progress and converted it into a point total, percentage, or grade, you must decide how to incorporate the grade into the calculation of the report card grade (see Chapter 11). One strategy involves using multiple grades for certain expectation areas (e.g., projects) in which the student practiced the skill and was assessed. For example, the individual points or grades the student earned on two projects could be

Table 16

Implementation Guide for Adaptations Involving Incorporating Progress on IEP Objectives

Adaptation	Preparing for Grading	Translating into Grades
Daily Work		
Base all or part of the grade on criteria established for an IEP objective.	1. Identify appropriate IEP objectives for grading. 2. Determine how progress will be measured and converted to a grade.	Determine if progress will serve as part of overall grade on an assignment, or if grade on assignment is based on criteria stated in objective.
Report Card Grades		
Base part of the grade on progress on an IEP objective.	1. Identify appropriate IEP objectives for grading. 2. Determine how progress will be measured and converted to a grade.	1. Determine whether progress grade is a separate grade combined with grades for other assignments in an expectation area. 2. Determine if progress is a separate expectation area that has its own weight (e.g., 20%) that it contributes to the report card grade. 3. Determine how progress will be measured and converted to a grade.

combined with the points or grade the student earned for progress on an IEP objective involving written expression. An alternative would be to consider progress on IEP objectives as a separate expectation area along with classwork, groupwork, projects, homework, and tests/quizzes, and

assigning progress its own weight (e.g., 15%) toward the report card grade.

Table 17 presents the evaluation matrix completed for grading adaptations involving progress on IEP objectives. Grading on progress will obviously produce a grade that accurately reflects progress on IEP objectives (#3). The extent to which other characteristics are present will depend on whether teachers arrange for the student to practice the skills addressed by the IEP objectives in the general education curriculum rather than supplemental materials. Further, the extent to which this adaptation produces grades that reflect student effort or that motivate the student to try hard will depend on the student's perceptions of the importance of IEP objectives. In general, teams must pay special attention to how this adaptation is implemented if effort and motivation are to be incorporated.

Because of the collaborative nature of IEP development and monitoring, an adaptation involving grading of progress is likely to produce collaboration between parents and teachers (#5) and between the special and general educator (#6), and result in coordination of the types and levels of supports provided in the general education classroom (#7). For this reason, this type of adaptation is recommended as a means to improve the overall services for students in inclusive classrooms. The impact on access to the general education curriculum (#8) will, of course, depend on the extent to which teachers provide the student opportunities within the general education curriculum to practice the skills described in the objective.

How fair students perceive grading on progress on IEP objectives to be may depend on their general knowledge of special education and why students have an IEP with individualized learning objectives. Other teachers may look for evidence that the objectives on which the student is being graded are challenging to the student and will lead to overall improvement in the quality of the student's work. Teams that are concerned about perceived fairness should look at how the classroom teacher individualizes expectations for all students, and how the teacher notes individual progress of each student.

Chapter Summary

This chapter described specific procedures for measuring progress on an IEP objective and incorporating progress into the grading system for an assignment or for an entire area for a marking period. Prior to implementing this adaptation, teachers must judge the accuracy of student's learning objectives and determine whether a student will have adequate opportunity to work on a given objective to warrant grading progress.

Table 17
Grading Adaptations Evaluation Matrix: Adaptations Incorporating Progress on IEP Objectives

Characteristic	Probable	Possible	Requires Special Attention	Comment
Effect on the Grade 1. Produces grades that accurately reflect progress on general education curriculum. 2. Produces grades that accurately reflect student effort and motivation. 3. Produces grades that accurately reflect progress on individual or IEP learning goals. 4. Produces grades that will motivate student to try hard in the future.	X	X	X X	1. Assumes that work on objectives occurs in general education curriculum. 2. Depends on student's motivation to make progress on IEP objectives. 3. Assumes that progress is measured accurately. 4. Depends on student's perceptions of importance of IEP objectives.
Effect on Grading Process 5. Results in collaboration between teachers and parents. 6. Results in collaboration between special and general educators. 7. Results in coordination of the classroom accommodations and how the student is graded. 8. Results in access to the general education curriculum.	X X X	X		5. Parents should be involved in decisions as part of IEP process. 6. Teachers should work together as part of the IEP process. 7. Decision to grade progress on objective(s) should result in clarification of types and levels of supports provided to student in general education classroom. 8. Depends on the extent to which student works in the general education classroom.
Effect on Community Perspectives 9. Perceived as fair by typical classmates. 10. Perceived as fair by other teachers.		X X		9. May be linked to students' general knowledge of the purpose of IEPs and why students have particular objectives. 10. May be influenced by the perceptions of validity of the IEP objectives and extent to which progress is linked to improvements in overall performance.

Indeed, the first step in grading progress may be overhauling the student's IEP so that the learning objectives reflect skills the student needs in the general education curriculum. Teachers are encouraged to be open-minded when approaching grading adaptations involving progress, and not to avoid such adaptations simply because they do not agree with the contents of the student's IEP.

Suggested Activities

The following activities are suggested for getting started on implementing grading adaptations involving measuring and grading of student progress on IEP objectives.

- Initiate a discussion between general and special educators regarding opportunities for students' IEP objectives to be addressed in the general education classroom. How this conversation unfolds will be determined by the structure of special education services in your school. For example, if the special educator typically supports students in a resource room or a study period, rather than in the general education classroom, this may be the first time the topic of implementing the IEP in the general education classroom is addressed.

- If you are a special educator, review the IEP objectives for your students and identify those that may be addressed in the curriculum and instruction in one or more general education classes. Realistically, any objective that focuses on a reading or writing skill can be addressed and measured on work in the general education curriculum. Consider how much easier and more accurate it may be to measure student progress on work in the general education classroom, where the student is generating products on a regular basis.

- If you are a general educator, review the IEPs for the students in your class, noting those that involve skills that the student needs to complete or work on in your class. Schedule a meeting with the special educator to discuss how you might address an objective in your class.

- Start small by focusing on just one objective for one student. This will allow you to determine how much instruction and assessment you already provide in your classroom lessons and routine, and what changes you would need to make to address the objectives. For example, you might start by focusing on an objective that involves answering literal comprehension questions from a textbook passage. Determine how you currently in-

struct students to read and compre-
hend their text and how you assess
their understanding. Consider
whether you devote enough time
to this skill so that the student with
this IEP objective could be expected to make progress, or
whether the student would require
some supplemental instruction,
perhaps on how to use a strategy
or an organizer. If more is needed,
consult with the special educator
about how more instruction can be
provided.

Where Do We Go From Here?

Thus far, procedures for implementing adaptations that involve
prioritization of content, adjusting a
balanced grading system, and grading progress on IEP objectives have
been presented. The next chapter proceeds to grading adaptations that involve measuring improvement.

CHAPTER 9
Measuring and Grading Improvement

This chapter will describe the following procedures for implementing grading adaptations that involve measuring improvement:

- Clarify what is meant by "improvement."

- Determine when a student may benefit from an adaptation involving improvement.

- Determine how to measure improvement and translate into a grade.

To understand specific grading adaptations, teams must first share a definition of "improvement" as it is used when discussing grading. Discussions of improvement in the professional literature and the way in which teachers in our research have described improvement suggest that "improvement" and "progress" are often used interchangeably, but indeed have different meanings. Following are common definitions and examples for the two terms.

Progress describes an increase in student knowledge or skills over time as a result of exposure to instruction or the opportunity to practice skills. Any amount of learning can be described as progress, even when more learning was expected. Progress can also be described as the amount of the content a student mastered during a marking period. Saying that a student "made good progress," is not describing the rate of new learning or the accurate use of skills. Thus, the term "progress" is not interchangeable with improvement as defined below.

Improvement describes an increase in the rate or amount of new learning or skill use over what was observed in the past. For example, we would say that a student "improved" in math class if he mastered a greater number of concepts or problem types than in previous marking periods. When students show improvement, it is often because they have worked harder, used different methods to complete their work, or received more effective instruction, supports, or materials. "Improvement" is not interchangeable with "progress" because it indicates an increase in rate of progress.

To summarize, there exists an important distinction between progress, which is reflected in the student's performance on assignments or IEP objectives, and improvement, which can be interpreted to mean an increase in performance that exceeds what would be expected, and that is most probably linked to student effort, improvements in instruction, and the student's increasing proficiency with processes.

For the purposes of making grading adaptations, adhering to the definition for improvement, not progress is recommended. A grading adaptation based on improvement should be designed to motivate the student to use all available supports and effort to increase progress and productivity on one or more types of assignments. In essence, a grading adaptation in which improvement is considered can serve as a challenge to students to exceed their rate or amount of progress or productivity over past levels.

Prior to integrating improvement into the grading system, the teacher or team must be certain that the student has the necessary background knowledge and skills, and the appropriate supports, to improve the student's performance. Offering to add bonus points if a student can raise test scores by 10% may backfire if the student lacks the abilities to raise the score. Some students can and do earn low grades because their disabilities are significant enough to affect their performance even with effective instruction and good effort. Thus, for some students, an offer of bonus points for increasing their test grades is just one more source of pressure. They may be saying to themselves, "If I could get a higher grade, don't you think I would!"

The present description of grading adaptations distinguishes progress from improvement, and focuses on the latter. Grading adaptations that focus on progress are also available. Progress can be described as the amount of classroom content or curriculum the student learns or masters. Generally, grading systems are designed primarily to measure progress, as discussed in the previous chapter on the role of products, processes, and effort in the balanced grading system. When a student makes minimal progress and earns a low grade, different strategies may be used to improve learning.

For example, the team may reconsider the types of supports that are being provided. If the supports seem to be appropriate, a grading adaptation may be considered to improve student performance on the classroom content. Several grading adaptations may be helpful, particularly those involving prioritization of content and related assignments, grading progress on IEP objectives, or grading process use.

Although the distinction between progress and improvement may seem a matter of semantics, a true distinction does exist when making grading adaptations. Teams are encouraged to discuss this difference with colleagues and team members as part of the preparation for making a grading adaptation based on improvement.

Tips from Teachers

Teachers participating in our research have implemented grading adaptations based on improvement, and our involvement with the teachers has suggested the following general guidelines.

• Select a performance (e.g., completing a project, completing homework, taking tests) for which the student possesses the skills and resources required to make significant improvement. The potential risk of offering bonus points or an increase in the grade to a student who can exert a superior effort but still falls short of the goal for improvement is serious, as such a case could lead to frustration, lowered perceived self-efficacy, and even distrust. In short, make certain a student is capable of making the targeted improvement before formalizing such a grading adaptation.

• Select a performance that is currently bringing down the student's grade. For example, if a student fails to complete 70% of homework assignments, and homework constitutes 20% of the student's report card grade, homework may be an area in which improvement could be targeted.

• Set challenging but obtainable goals for improvement. If the goal is too low, the student may achieve it easily, which may influence how peers and teachers perceive the "fairness" of the adaptation. The purpose of grading improvement is to motivate the student to work hard, which usually results in enhanced performance and higher grades. Once a student has made the targeted improvement, "naturally occurring" reinforcers such as social attention, higher grades, and elevated self-esteem and perceived self-efficacy should become available, and bonus points for improvement should no longer be necessary.

Tool 9-1 is designed to guide teams through the process of selecting performance areas in which grading improvement may be beneficial. The first column lists the performance areas in which performance is assessed and graded. In the second column you can describe the specific assignment if more than one occur in each performance area. For example, you may have two types of regular groupwork, laboratories and poster presentations, in your science class. If the student receives low grades in laboratories, you will write that in the box and move to the next column, which provides options for measuring improvement. Remember that you must select a student performance that can be measured. Examples from our research include increasing quiz scores and increasing the percentage of homework assignments completed. The last column is dedicated to converting the improvement into a grade. This step requires that the team set a clear goal for the student's performance. In an earlier example, a student completed 30% of homework assignments. The student's team may establish a goal of doubling completed assignments, with an incentive of 10 bonus points added to the student's homework grade if the student meets the goal.

Table 18 presents the implementation guide for adaptations involving measuring improvement. The final procedure for this adaptation involves determining whether the points/grades awarded for improvement should be attached to the assignment on which the improvement was noted, or added to the points/grades for an entire expectation area at the end of the marking period. An advantage of assigning bonus points or a grade for improvement on an individual assignment is that the student receives more immediate feedback than would be available if points or grades are added when the report card grade is being calculated. In general, students should receive feedback, including grades, as soon after they have completed their work as possible.

Table 19 presents the evaluation matrix completed for grading adaptations involving measuring improvement. The ratings we have assigned to grading on improvement reflect the reality that the impact of the adaptation depends on what skills we ask the student to improve. If the student improves on work in the general education curriculum, the resulting grade may reflect progress on the general education curriculum (#1), and the process will include access to the general education curriculum (#8). Producing a grade that reflects progress on IEP objectives (#3) would require that the student improve on specific objectives.

Tool 9-1
Pinpointing Areas in Which to Grade Improvement

Performance Area	Specific Assignment	Measure of Improvement	Converting Improvement to Grade
Classwork		___ higher score or points ___ occur more often ___ higher percentages ___ increased accuracy ___ other	
Homework		___ higher score or points ___ occur more often ___ higher percentages ___ increased accuracy ___ other	
Groupwork		___ higher score or points ___ occur more often ___ higher percentages ___ increased accuracy ___ other	
Test/Quiz		___ higher score or points ___ occur more often ___ higher percentages ___ increased accuracy ___ other	
Project		___ higher score or points ___ occur more often ___ higher percentages ___ increased accuracy ___ other	
Other		___ higher score or points ___ occur more often ___ higher percentages ___ increased accuracy ___ other	

Table 18
Implementation Guide for Adaptations Involving Measuring Improvement

Adaptation	Preparing for Grading	Translating into Grades
<u>Daily Work</u>		
Base all or part of the grade on improvement from past assignments.	1. Identify a specific area in which improvement will be graded. 2. Establish current level of performance and desired improvement. 3. Develop a scale for converting the level of improvement to a specified number of points or grade.	Determine if points or grade for improvement will be added to points/grade for an individual assignment, or if points/grade for improvement will be based on performance over the entire marking period and then added to total points/grades for an expectation area (e.g., tests/quizzes).
Assign bonus points for meeting or exceeding specified criteria.	Same as above except the team must establish a scale for awarding bonus points based on a specified level of improvement.	Same as above exept the decision is whether to add bonus points to an individual assignment or for improvement over the course of entire marking period.
<u>Report Card Grades</u>		
Base part of the grade on improvement over past work.	1. Identify a specific area in which improvement will be graded. 2. Establish current level of performance and desired improvement. 3. Develop a scale for concerting the level of improvement to a specified number of points/grade.	Determine if points/grade for improvement in a specified area will be combined with points/grades for individual assignments, or added to points/grades for the area when the report card grade is calculated at end of marking period.
Assign bonus points for meeting or exceeding specified criteria.	1. Same as above except the team must establish a scale for awarding bonus points based on a specified level of improvement.	Same as above except the decision is whether to add bonus points to an individual assignment or for improvement over the course of entire marking period.

The seeming strength of this adaptation is that improvement should reflect student effort (#2) and the student should be motivated to work hard knowing that improvement will be rewarded (#4). Another seeming benefit of grading on improvement is that the decision on what type of improvement to focus on is likely to require communication between the special and general educators regarding the role of the student's effort versus the student's skills and resources in improving performance. The special educator may be prepared to describe how the student's disabilities, and not effort, affect performance in the classroom. An ideal scenario is one in which the student's parents are invited to participate in design of the adaptation (#5).

How students and teachers will perceive this adaptation is difficult to gauge. Perceived fairness may be higher if the students observe the student working harder to make improvement. On the other hand, peers may also conclude that the student improved performance only when a special incentive was provided, which may cause them to see the adaptation as unfair, perhaps even deleterious to the student with the adaptation. As for perceptions of teachers, it seems that the above issues for students would also apply. The adaptation may be perceived as fairer if the student does improve performance and then maintains it without an adaptation.

Chapter Summary

This chapter described specific procedures for implementing grading adaptations that involve measuring and grading improvement. Prior to pursuing such an adaptation, teachers must clarify their definition of "improvement," as it is often confused with general progress. For the purpose of making grading adaptations, improvement has been defined as an increase in the rate of student learning, progress, or performance over past levels, attributable to improved instruction or increased student effort. Measuring and grading improvement requires establishing a "baseline" performance upon which to improve. Grading improvement is most beneficial for motivating the student to try hard.

Suggested Activities

The following activities are suggested for getting started on an adaptation involving grading of improvement:

- Initiate discussion with your colleagues about how they measure student improvement, and whether they consider improvement when grading.

Table 19
Grading Adaptations Evaluation Matrix: Adaptations Involving Measuring Improvement

Characteristic	Probable	Possible	Requires Special Attention	Comment
Effect on the Grade 1. Produces grades that accurately reflect progress on general education curriculum. 2. Produces grades that accurately reflect student effort and motivation. 3. Produces grades that accurately reflect progress on individual or IEP learning goals. 4. Produces grades that will motivate student to try hard in the future.	X (2) X (4)	X (1)	X (3)	1. Depends on whether improvement can be or is reflected in work products. 2. Assumes that improvement is due, at least in part, to student effort. 3. Would require that improvement be measured specifically on IEP objectives. 4. Assumes tht student has skills and resources to improve performance.
Effect on Grading Process 5. Results in collaboration between teachers and parents. 6. Results in collaboration between special and general educators. 7. Results in coordination of the classroom accommodations and how the student is graded. 8. Results in access to the general education curriculum.	X (6)	X (5) X (8)	X (7)	5. Depends on whether parent is involved in the design and monitoring of the adaptation. 6. Teachers should work together to set goals for improvement and determine whether student has abilities and resources to improve performance. 7. Possible if teachers revise supports to encourage student effort. 8. Depends on whether student is to improve work on general education curriculum.
Effect on Community Perspectives 9. Perceived as fair by typical classmates. 10. Perceived as fair by other teachers.		X (9) X (10)		9. May be enhanced if student improvement is obvious to peers. May be influenced by teacher attention to improvement of all students. 10. May be influenced by the extent to which improvement improves the student's general performance in the classroom.

- Review your school district's grading policy for information regarding specific adaptations, including those based on improvement. Most policies do not describe specific adaptations, and you may suggest to your colleagues that a committee pursue revisions.

- Start small by focusing on one student's improvement in one performance area. You may want to establish a contingency by which the student will earn bonus points or a higher grade for improving performance by a specified level. Consider asking the student to suggest goals for improvement.

Where Do We Go From Here?

The past four chapters have described procedures for grading adaptations that involve changing the types of student performances that will be graded. The three prior adaptations, as well as grading improvement, have the potential for changing the student's behavior by shifting focus to certain performances. The final adaptation involves shifting the scales and weights used to convert points or percentages to a letter grade. Such shifting does not necessarily promote a change in the student's performance, but rather, changes the way that the current performance is translated into a grade.

CHAPTER 10
Changing Scales and Weights

This chapter will describe the following procedures for implementing grading adaptations that involve changing scales and weights:

• Clarify your current grading scale and weighting of student performances.

.

• Determine when a student may benefit from a change in the scale and weights.

• Determine what changes should be made to the scale and weights.

The adaptations described in this chapter function differently than those presented in previous chapters in that they do not affect what expectations are placed on the student, or what types of performances will be graded. You could simply change the criteria and weights for grading an individual student while continuing to instruct and assess as before. The "action" in the adaptation occurs after the student has completed the assigned work and the teacher has evaluated the work and assigned a score, points, or percentages.

At this point, teams may make an adaptation by using a different scale for converting the score, points, or percentage to a grade, or by shifting the weight that certain assignments count toward a report card grade. An example of changing the grading scale might involve lowering the range of scores for a D to 60% from the 69% required in the schoolwide grading scale. You may choose to make such a change if the team decided that 69% is unobtainable for a particular student, because of the student's disability, but were confident that the student had acquired enough knowledge and skills to warrant a passing grade. This example may be provocative, particularly at a time when so-called social promotion is under fire.

Whether you consider the adaptation in the example to be "fair," probably depends on your experiences with students who have received failing grades and were forced to repeat a class. Your view of the fairness of changing the scale may also be different if the change allowed a student to earn an A rather than a B. The author encountered this scenario in schools where the criteria for an A had recently been raised from 90% to 93%, and the team felt that the student would never receive an A, regardless of how hard the student worked. Finally, your perception of changing the grading scale may also change depending on whether the change is for an individual assignment (e.g., tests) or report card grade.

Changing the weights for performance areas that count toward the report card grade presents issues similar to those for changing the grading scale. To clarify, weights refer to the percentage or proportion that a particular performance area (e.g., classwork, homework, groupwork, tests/quizzes, projects) contributes to the report card grade. For example, your classroom grading system may stipulate that 40% of the student's report card grade will be determined by the combined points, percentages, or grade for tests/quizzes. Perhaps another 30% of the report card grade will be determined by performance on a large project, with another 20% representing the student's main grade on homework assignments. The remaining 10% of the grade may come

from the student's response to classroom rules and behavioral expectations. Different combinations of weights have been used to determine a report card grade, but in general, the strategy for shifting weights from one performance area to another includes the following steps:

1. The team determines the student's overall grade, points, or percentages for each of the performance areas.

2. The team pinpoints the performance areas that produce low grades, points, or percentages to the student's overall report card grade.

3. The team considers each of the "low" performance areas to determine if the student's disability, rather than just effort, is the cause of lower performance.

4. The team considers shifting weight away from the areas that produce chronically low grades, points, or percentages to another performance area.

5. The team shifts the weight to a performance area in which the student can perform well if the student expends the necessary effort, and that allows the teacher to assess student learning.

The final step is important if the grade is to accurately reflect student performance on the general education curriculum. For example, a popular adaptation involving shifting of weights is to take weight from tests/quizzes and shift it to homework. Such a shifting meets criteria if the homework assignments require the student to demonstrate mastery on a sufficient portion of the classroom curriculum. However, it does not meet criteria if the shift is made just because the student performs poorly on tests/quizzes and the team shifted the weight to an area, such as homework, that can be completed outside of the classroom.

In general, teachers should consider changes to the grading scale or weights as temporary interventions that can be reconsidered periodically and continued as needed. Tool 10-1 is designed to guide the team through the steps for changing grading scales or weights. Note that the tool prompts the team to provide a rationale for any proposed changes. Teams are encouraged to be frank when describing your rationale, to prevent disappointment if the adaptation does not meet a team member's expectations. For example, you may wish to shift your weight for homework from 15% to 25% with the expectation that a student in your math class will be attempting more difficult homework

that will require more time and reliance on notes taken in class. Assuming the student performs well on the homework, you will be able to assess the student's understanding of the material, more validly than with a test. If the student and the student's parents do not see the purpose of the adaptation, they may be confused when the student ends up struggling more with homework, perhaps even earns lower grades on a few assignments. Perhaps they had anticipated that the grading adaptation would provide relief from test grades that always drag down the student's report card grades, overlooking the increased responsibilities for homework. Thus, it is important that team members understand the rationale for changing a grading scale or weights and communicate with the student and their parents.

Tips from Teachers

Teachers participating in our research have implemented grading adaptations involving changing scales and weights, and have offered the following observations and tips.

• Some parents and teachers are eager to change the grading scale to allow a student to earn a high grade and perhaps make the honor roll for the school. Although the merits of this application can be debated on philosophical grounds,

Tool 10-1
Changing Your Grading Scale or Weights

Current Grading Scales	Proposed Grading Scale	Rationale
Daily Assignments		
Report Cards		

Current Weights for Report Cards	Proposed Weights	Rationale
Classwork =		
Homework =		
Tests/Quizzes =		
Groupwork =		
Projects =		
Rules/Expectations =		
Other =		

changing the scale for this purpose is generally discouraged. The logic is that other types of adaptations (e.g., grading effort, grading process use) can be used to add points or percentages to a student's grade and thereby raise the grade to a higher level.

- Consider changing the grading scale or shifting weights as a means to "jumpstart" a student's performance. In several cases, teachers in our projects have lowered the grading scale for tests/quizzes so that a student could earn a D or a C after a marking period of failing grades. The teachers' rationale is that the student has given up after receiving a failing grade. Assuming that the student can and does achieve the lowered criteria, the teachers may raise the criteria to their original level in subsequent marking periods, after discussing the change with the student and the student's parents.

- Teachers who shift weights from one type of assignment (e.g., tests) to another (e.g., projects) usually, and appropriately, also adjust their expectations for those assignments. A common adaptation involves shifting weight away from tests/quizzes to projects or homework, based on the rationale that the stu-

dent has more time and "control" over the latter work. However, a shift in weight to those areas is usually accompanied by a discussion of the expectations for the student to complete the work as independently and accurately as possible. The message is clear: "I'll shift more weight to your homework, but I expect that you will do your very best work as part of that arrangement."

Table 20 presents the implementation guide for adaptations involving changing scale or weights. The procedures are straightforward and relatively easy because the "action" in the adaptation does not require any changes in the types of assignments that are given or the way in which they are graded. That is, you can retain your current grading criteria for assigning points or percentages, and then use your adapted scale to assign a grade. Similarly, you can maintain the same expectations and method of summing up points or percentages for report card grades. The change occurs when you convert the points/grades for individual expectation areas into a report card grade. Because changing your scale or weights does not involve a change in what you choose to grade or your criteria, it can be combined easily with other adaptations.

Table 20
Implementation Guide for Adaptations Involving Changes to Grading Scale or Weights

Adaptation	Preparing for Grading	Translating into Grades
Daily Work		
Change the number of points or percentages required to earn a specified letter grade on an assignment.	1. Clarify your current grading scale. 2. Use Tool 10-1 to identify a proposed scale and your rationale for making the change.	No special procedures are necessary to determine the grade once you have changed your scale or weights.
Report Card Grades		
1. Change the number of points or percentages required to earn a specified report card grade.	1. Clarify your current grading scale. 2. Use Tool 10-1 to identify a proposed scale and your rationale for making the change.	No special procedures are necessary to determine the grade once you have changed your scale or weights.
2. Change the weights assigned to different performance areas.	1. Clarify your current grading scale. 2. Use Tool 10-1 to identify a proposed scale and your rationale for making the change.	No special procedures are necessary to determine the grade once you have changed your scale or weights.

Table 21 presents the evaluation matrix for this type of grading adaptation. In general, adaptations involving changes in the scale or weights are initiated when a student receives chronically low or unsatisfactory grades and the team wishes to motivate the student to keep working hard, especially in areas of strength (#4).

The extent to which any other desirable characteristics are present depends on several factors, including the content and assignments for which the adaptation is made (#1, #8). The rationale for using this adaptation may be that a student can continue to be challenged in the general education curriculum without the risk

Table 21
Grading Adaptations Evaluation Matrix: Adaptations Involving Changes to Grading Scales and Weights

Characteristic	Probable	Possible	Require Special Attention	Comment
Effect on the Grade 1. Produces grades that accurately reflect progress on general education curriculum. 2. Produces grades that accurately reflect student effort and motivation. 3. Produces grades that accurately reflect progress on individual or IEP learning goals. 4. Produces grades that will motivate student to try hard in the future.	X	X X	X	1. Depends on whether expectations for working in general education curriculum remain unchanged by adaptation. 2. Assumes that student is motivated to work hard by the change in scale or weights. 3. Possible if weight is shifted to work that addresses an IEP objective. 4. Assumes that student is motivated by the opportunity to earn higher or more accurate grades.
Effect on Grading Process 5. Results in collaboration between teachers and parents. 6. Results in collaboration between special and general educators. 7. Results in coordination of the classroom accommodations and how the student is graded. 8. Results in access to the general education curriculum.		X X X	X	5. Possible if parents are invited to collaborate on the design and monitoring of the adaptation. 6. Teachers should collaborate to complete Tool 10-1. 7. This adaptation would not automatically require review of accommodations. 8. Depends on whether adaptation is made for general education curriculum and related assignments. Rationale for adaptation may be to maintain student in the general education curriculum without risk of failing grades.
Effect on Community Perspectives 9. Perceived as fair by typical classmates. 10. Perceived as fair by other teachers.			X X	9. May depend on students' perception that student is doing less but getting high grade. 10. May depend on perceptions that expectations has been reduced, or that student's responsibility to improve have been reduced.

or fear of failure. In this scenario, access to the curriculum will remain high, and peers and teachers would view the adaptation more fairly than if the student received the adaptation to work on content and assignments that were already significantly modified (#9, #10). Procedures for changing your scale or weights should involve collaboration between the special and general educators to complete Tool 10-1 (#6), and ideally involves input from the student's parents (#5). Although this adaptation can be made quite easily by the general educator, we urge that a team approach be used to ensure that the rationale for the adaptation is made clear.

In all likelihood, changing your scale or weights will not affect the degree to which the resulting grade reflects progress on IEP objectives (#3), nor will it lead to better coordination of accommodations for the student (#7). These additional desirable characteristics may be produced with special attention from the team, or more likely, by combining multiple adaptations into an individualized grading plan.

Chapter Summary

This chapter described specific procedures for implementing grading adaptations that involve changing the scales used to convert points or percentages to grades, or the weights that certain types of assignments or expectations count toward the report card grade. This type of adaptation should be used prudently, as it may not change the student's level of performance and may be perceived as less fair than other types of adaptations. Used appropriately, however, this adaptation can produce a grade that accurately reflects the type of work at which a student excels, and that can be used by the teacher to assess learning.

Suggested Activities

The following activities are suggested for getting started on an adaptation that involves changing scales and weights.

• Clarify the weights that you are currently using for your class. Consider whether students in your class seem to get low grades on certain types of assignments. Think about how you might change the weights to better reflect the amount of student learning and effort that is possible for different types of assignments. For example, if you believe that students learn as much from completing a project as they do by studying for and taking a test, you should weight the project equally or greater than the test.

- Review your grading policy for information on scales and weights. Grading scales are one type of information that is covered by most grading policies. Look for information about how and when the scale might be modified for certain students.

- Consider how clearly you have communicated your grading system, including the scale and weights, to your students and parents. Consider whether simply clarifying the weighting system might help students and their parents understand how the student is being graded.

- Initiate discussion with your colleagues about the potential benefits and perceived fairness of changing the grading scale or weights for students with disabilities. Such a discussion may lead to interest in developing more defined policies regarding grading adaptations in your school.

Where Do We Go From Here?

Having completed the how-to chapters for the five types of grading adaptations, the next chapter will discuss issues related to calculating and reporting student grades.

SECTION 4
Communicating Grading Adaptations

CHAPTER 11
Issues in Calculating and Reporting Student Grades

This chapter will discuss issues related to calculating and reporting grades for all students, including those with disabilities. Calculating and then reporting student grades can be done in different ways, but these do not represent grading adaptations. Calculating and reporting grades occur after the decisions about what and how to grade student work have been implemented.

This distinction is necessary because, in the author's experience, a significant number of teachers and administrators tend to focus on how their school calculates grades, their scale, and what information appears on their report card. Indeed, one of the most often questions we encounter is "What can be placed on the report card of a student with grading adaptations to note that different procedures were used?"

Hence, the author acknowledges the importance of these issues to teachers and administrators, and will

attempt in this chapter to discuss recommended practices. Although issues related to calculating and reporting grades are present for all students, special concerns or procedures will be noted for students who are receiving grading adaptations.

Issues in Calculating Grades

Several issues related to how grades are calculated are relevant to any discussion about grading systems for students with disabilities. Specific issues include methods for calculating grades based on multiple assignments, use of rubrics to evaluate student work and assign number or letter grades and use of electronic gradebooks.

How to Calculate

Calculating grades typically involves using a math computation to sum or average points or percentages. Most of us have used a "gradebook," often red, to record points or grades on student performances over the course of a marking period. At the end of the marking period we use our calculator to add points, or we average letter/number grades by assigning a point value (e.g., A = 4.0) and then averaging the points. When students fail to turn in an assignment, we might enter a "0" as a point or grade for uncompleted assignment.

Despite the widespread use of such practices, Guskey and Bailey (2001) have identified problems with these traditional methods to calculate grades, and recommend the following procedures be used to calculate grades for all students.

- Avoid averaging many scores collected over a long period of time, such as a marking period, to determine a report card grade. Doing so places too much emphasis on early scores that may not reflect how much the student learned by the end of the marking period. For example, if a student receives a low score on the first of 10 quizzes, that single score can make it impossible for the student to get an A, regardless of scores on the remaining nine quizzes. The authors recommend that we use the most recent scores when determining report card grades because they tend to be summative and reflect cumulative learning over the marking period. Another recommended practice is to use different types of perfor-

mances for grading, and avoid relying on one type of assessment that is repeated many times.

- Avoid assigning a "0" (zero) for work not completed because it does not reflect student achievement. While it may seem logical that students be penalized for not following instructions and completing work on time, the impact of "0"s on the student's overall grade is excessive. Alternatives to issuing a "0" include allowing the student more time to complete an assignment, or providing an alternative assignment with its own criteria for grading.

- Avoid deducting points for or lowering a grade because of problem classroom behavior, including poor attendance. In reality, problem behavior affects the ability of most students to perform well in class, thus their grades will already be depressed without an additional penalty. If a student's behavior is interfering with progress in class, developing a behavior management plan, rather than attempting to intervene through the grading system, is recommended.

A calculation issue related to grading adaptations is whether to apply an adaptation to individual assignments or when computing the report card grade. Adaptations that provide for grading of process use, effort, or improvement can be applied to individual assignments and will provide more immediate feedback to the student. For example, an adaptation in which a student receives points on each math homework assignment for showing all of the steps in a strategy should be implemented for each assignment, allowing the student to receive feedback on their performance before attempting the next assignment. As a result of our research, we recommend that, whenever possible, grading adaptations be applied to assignments.

Rubrics

Assigning points remains a popular method for evaluating student performance, despite criticisms that adding points to determine a grade often results in an inaccurate interpretation of performance (Marzano, 2000). Problems occur when points are averaged over several assignments, making it impossible for the student, teacher, or parents to interpret how the student performed on individual assignments. When points are translated into percentages (e.g., 80 out of 100 points equals 80%), the details of the students performance are further "hidden" and the resulting grade, often a B is assigned for 80%, holds little meaning.

An alternative scoring method is the rubric, which consists of a "set of scoring guidelines that describes a range of possible responses for a particular assessment item … and contains a scale that indicates the points that will be assigned to a student's work and a set of descriptors for each point on the scale" (Nolet & McLaughlin, 2000, p. 58). Points correspond to a set of quality descriptors for student work. One advantage of rubrics is that they require the teacher to clarify expectations for the student before an assignment is completed, which allows the student to do ongoing self-evaluation against the expectations while working.

Table 22 depicts a rubric for evaluating math problem solving from Nolet & McLaughlin (2000). Potential advantages of rubrics are that they allow evaluation of multiple dimensions or types of skills at the same time and therefore are useful for scoring complex assignments such as math problem solving, essay writing, or persuasive presentations.

Readers interested in learning more about rubrics are encouraged to read excellent texts by Marzano (2000), Nolet and McLaughlin (2000), or Thompson, Quenemoen, Thurlow, and Ysseldyke (2001), or access the following websites: http://www. rubistar.4teachers.org or http://

Table 22
Rubric for Scoring Math Problem-Solving

Score	Interpretation
4	• The student uses effective problem solving strategies and demonstrates a complete understanding of the dimensions of the problem. • No inaccuracies or computational errors are evident. • Data are well organized and displayed effectively. • All conclusions are based on data and logically supported with pertinent details.
3	• The student demonstrates a reasonable understanding of the problem and generally uses effective problem solving strategies. • Some minor errors or inaccuracies are present, but they do not affect the solution or conclusion. • Data are generally well organized and for the most part are displayed effectively. • Conclusions are generally supported by data and are logical.
2	• The student demonstrates an incomplete grasp of the problem but does attempt to use a problem solving strategy. • The problem contains substantial errors or inaccuracies that interfere with the solution. • Data are ineffectively organized or displayed. • Conclusions do not follow from data or are illogical.
1	• The student demonstrates a minimal understanding of the problem or uses an ineffective problem solving strategy. • Major errors or inaccuracies are present and interfere with the solution. • Data are poorly organized or displayed, or may not be displayed at all. • Conclusions are illogical or irrelevant.
0	No response or response is unacceptable.

Source: Nolet, V., & McLaughlin, M. J. (2000). *Accessing the general curriculum: Including students with disabilities in standards-based reform.* Thousand Oaks, CA: Corwin Press. Reprinted with permission of Corwin Press, Inc.

www.odyssey.on.cal~elaine.coxon/ rubrics.htm.

Grading adaptations are not incompatible with rubrics, which by design allow the teacher to evaluate different aspects of the student's performance. Rubrics for students with disabilities can be individualized to apply specifically to work that has been prioritized or that is related to an IEP goal. Although rubrics are generally used to score work products, they can be individualized to include a measure of process use, effort, or improvement. As is the case with any special procedures used for just one or a few students with disabilities, the team of student, parents, and teachers should collaborate to develop the procedure, which should be clearly described in the student's IEP.

Electronic Gradebooks and Systems

Computer-based grading systems for the individual classroom or an entire school or district have become increasingly popular due primarily to the perception that such systems are both efficient and accurate. We have conducted research in two schools using a districtwide electronic system in which teachers entered a grading scale and weights to be used for an entire class. Once scores had been input for all students, the grad-

ing program calculated the report card grade for each student. A perceived benefit of the system was that the teacher could assign weights to expectations (e.g., tests would equal 40%) of the student's grade, and the program would apply the weighting when calculating the grade. Administrators spoke favorably of the system because it created consistency across teachers and schools, and was an efficient way to produce report cards. Table 23 presents common electronic gradebooks and URLs to the companies websites where more information can be found.

While we appreciated the above benefits, we also noted potential problems associated with the electronic systems. First and foremost, the programs lacked flexibility in allowing different scales or weights for different students in the same class. As a result, students with personalized grading plans were required to be placed in a separate class in the program. While this was always achieved, we sensed that the extra step was considered a drawback of grading adaptations. In our current research, we address this issue immediately if a student's teacher or school uses an electronic system.

In his article, "Computerized Gradebooks and the Myth of Objectivity," Guskey (2002) alerts us to a tendency to confuse mathematical

Table 23
Electronic Gradebooks

Gradebook Name	Website Address
Altissima	http://www.habarbadi.com
A2Z Gradebook	http://www.a2zwaresolutions.com
Calico Educational Software	http://www.calicoed.com
Class Action Gradebook	http://www.classactiongradebook.com
Class Master	http://www.wkbradford.com
ClassRoom Windows	http://www.classroomwindows.com
Easy Grade Pro by Orbis Software	http://www.orbissoft
Easy Gradebook	http://www.hammersoftware.com
Excel-lent Gradebook	http://www.geocities.com
EZ Grader	http://www.ezgrader.com
Grade Book 1	http://www.fastrabbitsoftware.com
Gradebook 2.0	http://www.cchs.k12pa.us.com
Gradebook Power	http://www.gradebookpower.com
Grade Busters	http://www.gradebusters.com
Grade Genie	http://www.kilowattsoftware.com
Grade Guide	http://www.alberts.com
Gradekeeper	http://www.gradekeeper.com
Gradepoint	http://www.egradepoint.com
Grade Source	http://www.gradesource.com
Grade Star Gradebook	http://www.shelltech.com
J&D Gradebook	http://www.g-mark.com
Master Guide	http://www.maxium.com
Micro Grade	http://www.chariot.com
Grade Machine	http://www.mistycity.com
Grade Point	http://www.prime-fel.lvcm.com
The Pretty Good Grading Program	http://www.pggp.com
1st Class Grade Book	http://www.1st-class-software.com
Think Wave Educator Gradebook Software	http://www.thinkwave.com
Tiny Red Book: A Teachers Gradebook for Palm OS	http://www.tiny-red-book.com
VAR Grade 200, Verson 3.0	http://www.varedsw.com

precision with achieving accuracy and fairness in grading. Specifically, the author warns that a perception that grades computed by an electronic gradebook are inherently more accurate and defensible than those calculated using more traditional methods may be faulty in that the teacher must still exercise judgment when deciding what numbers and weights to place in the program. In addition, Guskey (2002) points out that electronic gradebooks may promote use of the strategies discouraged above, particularly averaging grades over an extended period of time and assigning zeroes for work not completed.

To summarize, we acknowledge that electronic grading systems present advantages to teachers and districts. Our recommendation is that teachers and administrators seek out programs that allow the maximum amount of flexibility for changing the grading system for individual students. And where systems lack such flexibility, we encourage teachers and administrators to avoid rejecting grading adaptations because they do not "fit" the electronic system.

Issues in Reporting Student Grades

The format in which student performance, including grades is reported has a significant bearing on how the information is received by students and parents (Guskey, 1996). As indicated in earlier chapters, parents have expressed dissatisfaction with the way in which their children's grades are reported. Following are recommended practices for report-ing grades for all students, and a specialized process for developing personalized grading plans for students with disabilities.

Methods for Reporting

In discussing how their child's progress is reported to them, most parents cite progress reports and report cards as the mechanisms for receiving information. In light of this tradition, progress reports and report cards will be discussed in more detail later. However, it must also be emphasized that no single mechanism is sufficient for communicating student achievement, and that progress reports and report cards cannot be expected to meet the expectations of students, parents, and teachers for communicating achievement. Table 24 presents a variety of mechanisms that might be included in a comprehensive reporting system (Guskey & Bailey, 2001, p. 176).

Discussion of each of the mechanisms is beyond the scope of this book. Readers are encouraged to read more about these options in the text cited above. As indicated earlier, progress reports and report cards are the most common mechanisms for reporting progress, and issues related to those traditions will be discussed in the next section.

Table 24
Mechanisms for Reporting Student Achievement and Progress

Official Documents
  • report cards
  • standardized assessment reports
  • weekly/monthly progress notes
  • newsletters to parents

Samples of Student Work
  • evaluated projects or assignments
  • portfolios

Events
  • school open-houses
  • parent-teacher conferences
  • student-teacher conferences
  • student led conferences

Informal communication
  • phone calls to parents
  • personal letters to parents

Electronic communications
  • school web pages
  • homework hotline

Adapted from: Guskey, T. R., & Bailey, J. M. (2001). *Developing grading and reporting systems for student learning*, p. 176. Thousand Oaks, CA: Corwin Press.

Progress Reports and Report Cards

The fact that no standardized format for progress reporting and report cards has been forwarded is testimony to the broad and complex expectations held by students, parents, and teachers for meaningful information on student achievement. Our own research has suggested that parents of secondary students view report card grades as ineffective at meeting a number of purposes, including communicating general achievement on the school curriculum or progress on individual learning objectives (Munk & Bursuck, 2001b).

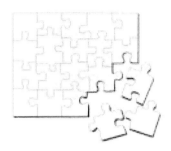

CHAPTER 12
A Model for Developing
Personalized Grading Plans
(PGPs)

For students receiving special education services, changes in the way that they will be graded must be described in their IEP. Our approach to meeting this requirement and promoting effective use and monitoring of grading adaptations has been to construct a Personalized Grading Plan (PGP) that becomes part of the student's existing IEP (Munk & Bursuck, 2001a, Munk, Bursuck, & Silvia, 2003). Tool 12-1 presents a suggested outline for a PGP, along with brief instructions and an example for "Olivia," for each section of the plan. The specific contents for the PGP have evolved to include a rationale for developing the PGP, a detailed description of the grading adaptations to be made, as well as the responsibilities for each team member in implementing the grading adaptations. While the PGP may seem to include more procedural detail than is typically found in an IEP, students, parents, and teachers in our projects have appreciated the detail.

We recommend that teams spend ample time determining and designing a progress reporting mechanism, with a first step of considering whether the reporting system for the school or classroom can be modified to include progress with the grading adaptations. In our experience, scheduling regular communication regarding progress with the grading adaptations results in improved communication about all matters of the student's education. Although the information needed to construct a personalized grading plan can be collected through individual contacts with the student, parents, and teachers, our experience suggests that a structured meeting of all team members generates the most productive discussion and results in a more effective PGP. Following is a description of the PGP process that we have implemented in our research on grading adaptations (Munk & Bursuck, 2001a; Munk et al., 2003).

The PGP Process

In our research on personalized grading plans, we have developed and refined the PGP process for collecting information, conducting a team discussion, and developing a personalized grading plan. Through tools and interviews, we collect the following types of input from each team member:

From the student

- Which classroom expectations (e.g., read and understand the materials) are most difficult to complete?

- What types of supports are provided by the student's teacher and parents?

- What would the student like grades to tell his teachers and parents?

From the parents

- Which classroom expectations are most difficult for their child to complete?

- What types of supports have been helpful in the past and in the current classroom?

- What types of assignments (e.g., homework) seem to drag their child's grades down?

- What purpose do they think that grades should serve?

From the special and general educators

- Which classroom expectations are most difficult for the student to complete?

- What types of supports are being provided as required by the IEP and what supports are being provided informally?

- What grades has the student received on types of assignments and on the report card?

- What types of assignments seem to drag the student's grade(s) down?

- What purpose(s) do they think that grades should serve?

- What type(s) of grading adaptation have the highest potential benefit for this student?

The PGP Meeting

The above information is collected prior to a meeting to discuss grading adaptations for the student. We have conducted special meetings as part of our research, but the same procedures could be implemented as part of the student's annual IEP review. Prior to beginning the process, a facilitator must be identified to lead the PGP meeting. The facilitator can be the special or general educator; however, we encourage the principal, social worker, psychologist, or another teacher to serve as the facilitator so that the teachers participating in the meeting do not have to be concerned about facilitating the discussion at the same time.

Prior to the PGP meeting, the parents receive a packet of information that describes the purpose of the PGP process and what they can expect to happen. The packet includes an overview of grading adaptations that is written in non-technical language and includes familiar examples. Parents are encouraged to review the overview and to identify adaptations that have the potential to help their child. Teachers receive a "prep packet" that includes a more thorough description of each type of adaptation and tools for planning the adaptations. Once the teachers have reviewed the adaptations and tools, they rate each type of adaptation using the tool we described in Chapter 5 and return the ratings to the facilitator.

The information collected prior to the meeting is summarized on a series of large laminated posters that can be erased for repeated use. Individual posters present the following information:

1. A welcome and description of what will occur during and after the meeting.

2. A summary of the student's strengths and challenges as reported by each team member and the supports being provided.

3. A summary of the perceived purposes for grades reported by the team members.

4. An overview of types of grading adaptations with a notation of those identified by the teachers as having potential benefit for the student.

5. A worksheet designed to guide the team through the development of the specific adaptation(s) they have selected.

As the facilitator guides the team through the posters, discussion may occur at any point, but generally occurs during the summarization of the student's challenges, the purposes for grades, and the evaluation and selection of a specific adaptation. The facilitator should encourage group members to discuss their views and rationale with each other, with a goal of reaching consensus whenever possible. However, the team need not reach complete agreement on any issue except the actual adaptation(s) to be implemented.

In our experience, the student and parents require more support and encouragement to express their views in the PGP meeting, and the facilitator must be careful not to assume that quiet means agreement. Many students and parents are not accustomed to being asked their opinion about grading, and may not be sure how to participate in the discussion. The refinements we have made in the PGP process and involved materials have been driven primarily by a desire to prepare the student, teachers, and parents to participate in a fruitful discussion once they are together.

More information about the PGP process may be found at our project web site:

http://www.cedu.niu.edu/projectpgp/

Chapter Summary

This chapter described a research-based model for developing personalized grading plans. The PGP model incorporates the concepts and strategies into a series of steps and activities that can be completed by school teams. Although development of personalized grading plans requires planned collaboration between student, parents and teachers, the benefits warrant the time and effort, especially for students with histories of chronic low or inaccurate grades.

Where do We Go From Here

By this point in the book, readers should have an appreciation for the complexities and pervasiveness of grading issues. But just in case some readers are skeptical about the significance of grading in contemporary society, the next chapter presents clear evidence from the media that these issues are alive and impacting many communities.

Tool 12-1
Outline for Personalized Grading Plan

Following is a suggested outline for writing a Personalized Grading Plan. The key components of the plan are numbered and appear in **bold**. Directions appear in normal text. Sample responses appear in *italics*.

---

1. Student name

> Olivia's PGP:
> *Olivia*

2. Classes addressed by PGP

The PGP process may involve one or more general education classes. All classes in which the PGP will be implemented must be listed here.

> Olivia's PGP:
> *For Olivia, the PGP process was used for only the science class. Therefore, the PGP will be implemented for science class.*

3. Rationale for developing PGP

We suggest that the team include a description of their rationale for implementing grading adaptations. A rationale serves as a reminder to present team members why they pursued a PGP for the student and provides important background information for the student's future educators who may encounter the PGP directly through interactions with the student, parent, or present educators, or indirectly through a review of the student's file.

The rationale might be thought of as a statement of a problem for which the PGP process was the intervention. Following are common problems or issues that might serve as a rationale for implementing the PGP process:

- The student has received or is receiving a low or failing grade(s) in one or more classes

---

- One or more team members has expressed an interest in discussing ways to help the student be more successful in one or more classes
- One or more team members has expressed dissatisfaction with the way the student is being graded
- Confusion regarding how the student is being graded seems to persist despite efforts to clarify the process
- Educators are currently using grading adaptations informally and wish to formalize the adaptations
- The school grading policy requires documentation when a grading adaptation is to be used
- Team members have expressed different perceptions of the purposes of grades
- Supports that have been recommended by the parents or educators may affect the student's options for future classwork or postsecondary careers

> Olivia's PGP:
> *The rationale for implementing the PGP process for Olivia was that she had received a low grade, D, in science in the prior marking period, and that Olivia and her mother had expressed concerns that the way in which Olivia was being graded may not be fair.*

4. Description of grading adaptations to be implemented

A description of the grading adaptation to be made must include the name of the grading adaptation, a precise description of how the adaptation will be made, and how the adaptation will impact the existing grading process for daily work or the way that report card grades are computed. The team should attempt to work out all the details of each grading adaptation at the PGP meeting, rather than leaving some details to be figured out by the educators after the meeting.

Tool 12-1 continued

Olivia's PGP:

Adaptations for Grading Daily Work

Base part of grade(s) on processes Olivia uses to complete her work: *For assignments that result in a written product that Olivia turns in for grading, she will receive a product grade as she has in the past, but will also receive a process grade based on her accurate use of the writing and editing strategies she has learned. The steps in each of the strategies will be made into a checklist so Olivia can check off each step as she completes it. For each assignment in which Olivia is to use the strategies, she will complete the checklist and then describe to the special educator how she used the steps to complete her written product. The special educator will initial the checklist verifying that Olivia used it to complete the work. Olivia will hand in the completed strategy checklists with her work products to the science educator. Completed checklists will comprise 20% of Olivia's grade on written assignments. For example, if a writing assignment is worth 100 points, Olivia will earn 20 of those points by completing the strategy checklists. The remaining criteria for the assignment will be 80 points, rather than 100 points.*

Adaptations for Determining the Report Card Grade

Base part of Olivia's grade on progress on IEP objective(s): *Part of Olivia's grade will be based on her performance on her IEP objective for using her assignment notebook to organize assignments and work. This objective will be addressed during the weather unit, during which Olivia will record the daily measurements on a spreadsheet and mark the daily measurements on a graph. Each measurement or graphed data point will be considered an "entry." She will record all entries each day with no prompting from either educator. The science educator* *will check Olivia's spreadsheet at the end of each class period and will circle any cells where entries are missing. Twenty percent (20%) of Olivia's classwork grade will be comprised of her grade for the spreadsheet and graph. She will drop one half grade (e.g., from an A to an A-) for each missed entry.*

5. Description of responsibilities for student, parents, and teachers in implementing the PGP

The specific responsibilities for the student, parents, general educator, and special educator should be listed with enough detail so that the team can determine if responsibilities are met. Responsibilities typically exist for the following aspects of the PGP:

1. Developing or procuring materials (e.g., organizers, checklists) required to implement the PGP.
2. Providing direct instruction to the student on materials, tools, or technology that the student is expected to use as part of the PGP.
3. Monitoring the effects of the PGP and reporting any concerns or problems to the team members.
4. Maintaining ongoing communication regarding the PGP.

Olivia's PGP:

We would describe the following responsibilities for team members:

Special Educator
1. *Develop the strategy checklists and instruct Olivia on how to use them.*
2. *Observe checklists and written work and check if Olivia used strategies effectively.*
3. *Collaborate with science educator to create spreadsheet and graphs for weather unit.*

Science Educator
1. *Inform special educator of written assignments for marking period.*
2. *Assign grades for completed strategy checklists.*
3. *Collaborate with special educator to create spreadsheet and graphs for weather unit.*
4. *Check Olivia's spreadsheet at the end of each class period during weather unit and circle missing entries.*
5. *Assign grade for spreadsheet and graphs at end of weather unit.*

Olivia
1. *Tell her teachers if she does not understand what she is supposed to do.*
2. *Tell her teachers if she does not think her PGP is helping her in the science class.*

Parents
1. *Contact the science or special educator if Olivia does not understand her PGP.*
2. *Report any concerns to the science or special educator immediately.*

6. Plan for monitoring plan and reporting progress to team members

We suggest that teams establish how they will communicate progress or problems with the PGP at the time of the PGP meeting. The team should decide how often they want to review progress on the PGP and whether they will communicate through informal or formal modes.

Olivia's PGP:
The team noted that Olivia's school already issues biweekly progress notes that provide general information on student progress in each class, as well as the number of absences for the period. Olivia's mother requested more specific information about how Olivia was performing with her PGP so that she could provide more help at home or just remind Olivia of what she was

Tool 12-1 continued

supposed to do. The team discussed simply exchanging phone calls biweekly, but decided that it was very difficult to make contact and would result in exchanging recorded messages. Therefore, the team decided that adding more information regarding the PGP to the biweekly progress notes would be satisfactory.

The team developed the following brief form to be completed by the teachers and initialed and returned by Olivia's mother.

PGP Progress Monitoring Note for Olivia

Date:_____

Completed by teachers

Grading Adaptations	Chances to Use in Last Two Weeks	Actually Used ____ Times	Possible Points Earned for Using Strategies
1. Use writing planning strategy and have completed checklist checked by teacher.			all some most
2. Use editing strategy and have completed checklist checked by teacher.			all some most
3. Complete spreadsheet accurately and have checked by teacher.			all some most

Completed by Olivia's parent

My initial here indicates that I have reviewed the progress note: _____

At this time, I think we should: ___continue the PGP as currently written
___ talk about minor concerns I have with the PGP
___ have a team meeting to review the PGP

Signatures

The PGP is signed by all team members, including the student.

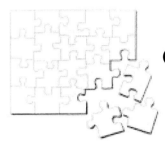

CHAPTER 13
Grading Issues in the News

Chapter 2 presented grading issues described in the educational literature to establish the need for innovation in grading practices. The presumption was that research and perspectives published in professional publications would be considered as accurate and credible to most readers. Even though most readers will have personal knowledge of grading issues, and perhaps even strategies for addressing those issues, they may not be aware of the universality of those issues among students, parents, and teachers.

Newspaper articles provide another source of evidence that grading issues persist across schools, states, and countries. Although perceived as less scholarly than professional journals, newspapers can provide more timely information, and in many instances can focus attention on the differing perspectives of community members and stakeholders. In the case of grading issues, newspapers may provide a glimpse into what local educators, administrators, students, and parents think is best practice.

This final chapter will present a sample of newspaper articles that focus on a grading issue. Following each article is a brief reflection linking the issues in the article to those in this text.

Issue: Report Cards can Communicate Different Types of Information

Calls for changes in report cards generally stem from concerns regarding the meaningfulness of the information, or the clarity with which it is presented. For example, parents may criticize report cards as not providing the type of information they find useful, or they may cite difficulty in reading, understanding, or interpreting the information on the report card. Regardless of the precise issue, report cards remain the most reported grading-related topic in the news.

The *Chicago Tribune* published a story entitled, "Should they get an A for effort," (2003, May 11) reporting that "after four years of work by parents, teachers, and administrators to come up with a grading system for report card grades," the school board for a northern suburb of Chicago rejected their proposal. At issue was the numerical system that would be used to indicate a student's progress toward learning standards for his/her grade level. The highest number, 4, would indicate that the student had "exceeded standards," while a grade of 2 would mean that the student was meeting standards "with support." According to the report, some school board members described aspects of the proposed numerical system as "befuddling" or "wishy-washy." This story is interesting in that it involves a seemingly collaborative effort to develop a grading system that is acceptable to teachers, parents, and administrators. Yet the committee was unable to generate a system that was perceived to be clear and meaningful.

In another example of innovation to improve the usefulness of report cards, the Chicago Public Schools have expanded the information reported on cards to include "a student's character development and an improvement plan for those struggling academically" ("New Data on Report Card Grades in Chicago," 2002). A consulting firm worked with the school district to develop the more comprehensive report card. In addition to the report card changes, school officials indicated that "there will be more uniformity in the grading scale." For example, percentages will be standardized so that an A at one school will be the same as an A at another school. Clearly, Chicago Public Schools are responding to the common criticism from parents that they do not receive enough information about their children's performance.

What is not clear from the article is how the district decided what type of information should be included in the new report cards; were decisions made by a committee of school personnel and parents, or by school personnel and the consulting firm? The statement from a school official indicating "more uniformity in the grading scale" denotes an underlying perception regarding the purpose of grades. For there to be such uniformity, grades would have to be based solely on student performance on a common classroom curriculum and assignments. What we cannot ascertain from the report is whether such uniformity is desired for students with disabilities, and if such a hypothetical grading policy would allow for grading adaptations for students with disabilities.

Innovation in report card systems has occurred in Canada, where Ontario schools have implemented a "standardized report card system" in which students in grades 1-6 receive letter grades, while those in grades 7-high school receive percentage marks ("New Grading Gets Poor Parental Marks," 2001). "The new format came in answer to parents who sought clear, detailed information about their children's progress," stated a spokesperson for the Education Ministry. The article included several skeptical comments by unidentified sources, with one quote reflecting the issues of purpose for and impact of grades: "If you don't have a child affected by the new letter grades, you might ask why people are so stressed out about it. But if you have a child in Grade 1 whose first ever report card grade contains a C in reading because he's just learning to read, you can begin to understand the upset. Those letters are highly symbolic to a parent and it's hard not to telegraph concern or disappointment to a child." Use of term "symbolic" in this quote suggests the power of grades to communicate different messages and to elicit an emotional response from students and parents.

Reflecting on the News

The above articles involve several links to the content of this book:

- The call for innovation in how report card grades are determined and reported continues, and communities seek to improve their systems in different ways.

- Proposed innovations focus primarily on standardization and uniformity, and do not seem to acknowledge issues for students with disabilities, or the existence of grading adaptations.

- Reports do not indicate systematic attempts by communities to clarify purposes for grades, or to clarify philosophical issues regarding individualization or fairness prior to developing a system.

Sources

Cholo, A.B. (2002, November 9). New data on report cards in Chicago. *Chicago Tribune*, p. 21.

New grading gets poor parental marks (2003, March 26). *Toronto Star*, p. L102.

Should they get an "A" for effort? (2003, May 11). *Chicago Tribune*, p. 2.

Issue: Alternatives to Letters/Numerals on Report Cards

In her story entitled, "U-46 Getting Ready to Leave A's and B's Behind New Standards-Based Reporting System Would do Away with Traditional School Grade," writer Naomi Dillon (2003) reports that the district will redesign its report cards to report progress on each of the Illinois Learning Standards. According to the report, "A sample report card would feature a separate page for each subject with the state goals and the measurements which teachers use to determine performance in that category. As they do in annual state tests, students would receive 'does not meet,' 'meets,' or 'exceeds' marks for each of the benchmarks." This report describes an alternative to letter/numerical grades that is an outgrowth of the standards-based movement.

Several Wisconsin schools are also reportedly abandoning letter grades in favor of terms such as "beginning" that are intended to describe progress toward specific learning standards ("Schools Sending Home a New Breed of Report Card," 2002). In an example reported for Madison Schools, the new model is "common to all schools," and will "categorize" student performance along the same lines – minimal, basic, proficient, or advanced – as the state's standardized test.

Reflecting on the News

The above articles involve several links to the content of this book:

- The above innovations provide further evidence of skepticism regarding the ability of letter/numerical grades to adequately describe student progress.

- In these examples, the report card resembles a checklist of learning objectives, or competencies, and teachers check a coded box to indicate progress toward meeting the objective. Such a system clearly reflects a perception that grades should be based on mastery of content.

- As is typical, students with disabilities are not addressed in the report, and we cannot ascertain whether the proposed grading systems would allow for individualization.

Sources

Dillon, N (2002, September 10). U-46 getting ready to leave the A's'and B's behind: New standards-based reporting system would do away with traditional school grades. *Daily Herald*, p. 6.

Hetzner, A. (2002, November 19). Schools sending home a new breed of report card: *Milwaukee Journal Sentinel*.

Issue: Bias in a Grading System

Chapter 3 discussed the perceived fairness of individualized grading strategies and concluded that the perceivers definition of "fair" and the way in which an adaptation is used can influence an ultimate judgment of fairness. That is, there is no formula for achieving fairness, nor can we predict how students, parents, and teachers will perceive an adaptation. Therefore, we can say that grading adaptations do not result in predictable bias against any student.

But suppose there is inherent and predictable bias in a schoolwide grading system, as has been argued in two separate cases in the news. The Wisconsin Department of Public Instruction received a complaint that a local high school's new grading policy discriminates against boys ("State Probing Complaint of Grading Bias Against Boys, " 2003). The complaint stems from a new grading system that, according to the complaint, " raised and standardized criteria for getting, say, an A or a B and added the use of pluses and minuses, hindering boys ability to compete for top grades and higher class rankings." Evidence for this bias included a drop in the "perfect-grade honor roll," and a small minority of boys in the National Honor Society. According to the report, some parents and the school principal believe that because boys are more likely to "challenge the teachers" and to have attention problems, they are not able to earn the top grades under the new system. Underlying this grading issue may be a larger issue of gender equity or privilege in schools.

To this author's knowledge, no one has forwarded a similar argument that grading systems are inherently biased against students with disabilities because they are less likely to achieve high grades and compete for class honors, nor does such an argument seem as fitting as that for gender bias. Yet, the issue of the "inclusiveness" of a grading policy is relevant for students with disabilities and could support more effective use of grading adaptations. While the above article does not provide scientific evidence for the purported differences in the behavior of boys, it does present arguments suggesting that grading systems should maintain enough flexibility to accommodate student differences.

In a second case from New Jersey ("Girl Takes Legal Action to be Valedictorian," 2003), a high school senior who received accommodations due to her immune deficiency disorder has asked a federal judge to prevent her school from forcing her to share the valedictorian honor with other students. Due to her disability, the student "has taken a class load that doesn't include physical education and involves her spending part of her school day studying at home." Because other students had to take gym classes that are weighted less toward their GPA, they ended up with slightly lower GPA's than the complaintant did. In explaining his rationale for the sharing of the award, the superintendent for the district said," After reviewing these issues, I was concerned about the fundamental fairness of the academic competition engaged in for the valedictorian and salutatorian awards." This case clearly reflects the significance of grades for high-achieving students. In this rare story regarding a student with a disability, the issue of whether legally mandated accommodations present an unfair advantage may be decided in court, and may have widespread implications for grading issues of students with disabilities. We will keep an eye on this case.

Reflecting on the News

The above stories have links to the contents of this book:

- Both stories focus on issues of fairness or bias for relatively high-achieving students, thus illustrating that grading issues exist for all students, and not just for those with low or failing grades.

- The goal in both stories is for the complainants to receive higher grades and be eligible for honors. Throughout this book, we have argued that an effective grading system produces grades that are fair and meaningful, and not necessarily high. The story from New Jersey focuses on how GPA's are calculated, and does not delve into the deeper issues about fairness and judgment. We might infer from the Wisconsin story that grading criteria should "relaxed" to accommodate boys, or that grades should be based on different criteria.

Sources

Girl takes legal action to be valedictorian. (2003, May 3). *Milwaukee Journal Sentinel*, p. 3A.

Johnson, A. (2003, April 28). State probes complaint of grading bias against boys. *Milwaukee Journal Sentinel*, p. B1.

Issue: Should Parents Receive Grades?

We have included this report to illustrate how embedded grades are in our school culture. A Pennsylvania school district is proposing report cards on which parents would receive a "yes" or "no" for "attendance at parent-teacher conferences, whether they return things they have to sign and whether their children come to school healthy and properly dressed" ("Proposal Would Make Sure Parents are Making Grade," 2003). According to the school's superintendent, "We have a lot of parents who are involved and do a wonderful job, but we need to make sure that it's widespread."

Clearly the proposers of the report card for parents perceive grading as a strategy for motivating parents to improve their performance on a set of indicators identified by the school district. What's not clear from the article is whether the competencies on the report cards were chosen collaboratively by students, parents, or teachers, or whether the district has considered lifestyle challenges and issues of poverty that might affect parent interaction with their children's school. Might we see calls for improving the accuracy and meaningfulness of parent report cards in the future?

Reflecting on the News

The above story has links to the contents of this book:

- The stated purpose for the parent report card is to acknowledge those who fulfill responsibilities and to encourage those who do not. The supporters are assuming that symbols or grades can motivate parents to meet expectations.

- The fact that parents would be provided feedback in the form of a report card indicates how ingrained this practice is in American schools.

Source

Proposal would make sure parents are making grade. (2003, February 10). *Chicago Tribune*, p. 36.

Sharpening Your Eye for Grading Issues in the News

The purpose of this book has been to sensitize readers to the many issues surrounding grading for all students, and particularly for those with disabilities. As a result of this awareness, you may find yourself focusing more attention on grading issues in your local community. Following are questions to ask as you consider new developments on grading related issues.

- Does the grading issue involve students with disabilities and, if not, are there potential implications for these students?

- Does the grading issue involve underlying beliefs about the purpose for or meaning of grades?

- Do parties involved with issue seem to have a clear, if unstated, perception of what criteria grades should be based on?

- Do parties involved with the issue seem to be advocating for teacher judgment or individualization in grading systems?

- Is the grading issue related primarily to how performance is reported, with little or no concern with how grades are determined on a day-to-day basis?

By asking these questions, you will be able to identify situations in which issues could be resolved by expanding knowledge of the purposes for grades and strategies for making grading systems effective for blended classrooms and individual students. As we stated earlier, we all can claim some expertise in grading student performance, and for that reason, a collaborative approach to generating solutions is our best hope for the future.

References

Azwell, T., & Schmar, E. (1995). *Report card on report cards: Alternatives to consider.* Portsmouth, NH: Heinemann.

Bateman, B. D., & Linden, M. A. (1998). *Better IEPs: How to develop legally correct and educationally useful progress* (3rd ed.). Longmont, CO: Sopris West.

Bietau, L. (1995). Student, parent, teacher collaboration. In T. Azwell & E. Schmar (Eds.), *Report card on report cards: Alternatives to consider* (pp. 11-21). Portsmouth, NH: Heinemann.

Bradley, D. F., & Calvin, M. P. (1998). Grading modified assignments: Equity or compromise. *Teaching Exceptional Children, 21,* 24-29.

Bursuck, W. D., Munk, D. D., & Olson, M. M. (1999). The fairness of report card grading adaptations: What do students with and without disabilities think? *Remedial and Special Education, 20,* 84-92.

Bursuck, W. D., Polloway, E. A., Plante, L., Epstein, M. H., Jayanthi, M., & McConeghy, J. (1996). Report card grading and adaptations: A national survey of classroom practices. *Exceptional Children, 62,* 301-318.

Calhoun, M. L. (1986). Interpreting report card grades in secondary schools: Perceptions of handicapped and nonhandicapped students. *Diagnostique, 16,* 117-124.

Carpenter, D. C. (1985). Grading handicapped pupils: Review and position statement. *Remedial and Special Education, 6,* 54-59.

Chandler, H. N. (1983). Making the grade. *Journal of Learning Disabilities, 16,* 241-242.

Christiansen, J., & Vogel, J. R. (1998). A decision model for grading students with disabilities. *Teaching Exceptional Children, 31*(2), 30-35.

Cohen, S. B. (1983). Assigning report card grades to the mainstreamed child. *Teaching Exceptional Children, 15,* 86-89.

Deshler, D. D., Ellis, E. S., & Lenz, B. K. (1996). *Teaching adolescents with learning disabilities: Strategies and methods* (2nd ed.). Denver, CO: Love.

Donohoe, K., & Zigmond, N. (1990). Academic grades of ninth-grade urban learning disabled students and low-achieving peers. *Exceptionality, 1,* 17-27.

Drucker, H., & Hansen, B. C. (1982). Grading the mainstreamed handicapped: Issues and suggestions for the regular social studies classroom teacher. *The Social Studies, 73,* 250-251.

Durm, M. W. (1993). An A is not an A is not an A: A history of grading. *The Educational Forum, 57,* 294-297.

Edyburn, D. (2002). Technology integration. *Special Education Technology Practice, 4*(1), 16-28.

Friedman, S. J., & Truog, A. L. (1999, Summer). Evolution of high school teacher's written grading policies. *ERS Spectrum.*

Friend, M., & Bursuck, W. D. (2002). *Including students with special needs: A practical guide for classroom teachers* (3rd ed.). Needham Heights, MA: Allyn & Bacon.

Friend, M., & Cook, L. C. (1996). *Interactions: Collaboration skills for school professionals* (2nd ed.). White Plains, NY: Longman.

Frierson, E. C. (1975). *Grading without judgement: A classroom guide to grades and individual evaluation.* Nashville, TN: EDCOA Publications.

Frisbie, D. A., & Waltman, K. K. (1992). Developing a personal grading plan. *Educational Measurement: Issues and Practice, 11*(3), 45-52.

Gersten, R., Vaughn, S., & Brengelman, S. V. (1996). Grading and academic feedback for special education students with learning difficulties. In T. R. Guskey (Ed.), *Communicating student learning: 1996 yearbook of the association for supervision and curriculum development* (pp. 47-57). Alexandria, VA: Association for Supervision and Curriculum Development.

Guskey, T. R. (2002, June). Computerized gradebooks and the myth of objectivity. *Phi Delta Kappan, 83,* 775-780.

Guskey, T. R., & Bailey, J. M. (2001). *Developing grading and reporting systems for student learning.* Thousand Oaks, CA: Corwin Press.

Guskey, T.R. (1996). *Communicating student learning: 1996 yearbook of the association for supervision and curriculum development.* Alexandria. VA: Association for Supervision and Curriculum Development.

Haladyna, T. M. (1999). *A complete guide to student grading.* Boston: Allyn & Bacon.

Hasselbring, T. S. (2001). A possible future of special education technology. *Journal of Special Education Technology, 16,* 15-21.

Hendrickson, J., & Gable, R. A. (1997). Collaborative assessment of student with diverse needs: Equitable, accountable, and effective grading. *Preventing School Failure, 41,* 159-163.

Horowitz, S. (1982). Developing a junior high school or middle school resource program. In J. H. Cohen (Ed.), *Handbook of resource room teaching* (pp. 139-168). Rockville, MD: Aspen Systems.

Juarez, T. (1994). Mastery grading to serve student learning in the middle grades. *Middle School Journal, 26,* 37-41.

King-Sears, M. (2001). Three steps for gaining access to the general education curriculum for learners with disabilities. *Intervention in School & Clinic, 37*(2), 67-76.

Lieberman, L. M. (1982). Grades. *Journal of Learning Disabilities, 15,* 381-382.

Lindsey, J. D., Burns, J., & Guthrie, J. D. (1984). Intervention grading and secondary learning disabled students. *The High School Journal, 67,* 150-157.

Marzano, R. J. (2000). *Transforming classroom grading.* Alexandria, VA: Association for Supervision and Curriculum Development.

Mehring, T. (1995). Report card options for students with disabilities in general education: In T. Azwell & E. Schmar (Eds.), *Report card on report cards: Alternatives to consider* (pp. 131-153). Portsmouth, NH: Heineman.

Munk, D. D., & Bursuck, W. D. (1998a). Can grades be helpful and fair? *Educational Leadership, 55,* 44-47.

Munk, D. D., & Bursuck, W. D. (1998b). Report card grading adaptations for students with disabilities. Types and acceptability: *Intervention in School and Clinic, 33,* 306-308.

Munk, D. D., & Bursuck, W. D. (2001a). Preliminary findings of personalized grading plans for middle school students with disabilities. *Exceptional Children, 67,* 211-234.

Munk, D. & Bursuck, W.D. (2001b). What report card grades should and do communicate: Perceptions of parents of secondary students with and without disabilities. *Remedial and Special Education, 22,* 280-286.

Munk, D. D., Bursuck, W. D., & Silva, M. (2003). *Personalized grading plans for included middle school students with disabilities.* Manuscript in progress.

Nolet, V., & McLaughlin, M. J. (2000). *Accessing the general curriculum: Including students with disabilities in standards-based reform.* Thousand Oaks: Corwin Press.

Ornstein, A. C. (1994). Grading practices and policies: An overview and some suggestions. *NASP Bulletin, 78,* 55-64.

Polloway, E. A., Bursuck, W. D., Jayanthi, M., Epstein, M. H., & Nelson, J. S. (1996). Treatment acceptability: Determining appropriate interventions within inclusive classrooms. *Intervention in School and Clinic, 31*, 133-144.

Polloway, E. A., Epstein, M. H., Bursuck, W. D., Rodrique, T. W., McConeghy, J. L., & Jayanthi, M. (1994). Classroom grading: A national survey of policies. *Remedial and Special Education, 15*, 162-170.

Pugach, M. C., & Warger, C. L. (2001). Curriculum matters: Raising expectations for students with disabilities. *Remedial and Special Education, 22*, 194-196.

Rojewski, J. W., Pollard, R. P., & Meers, G. D. (1992). Grading secondary vocational education students with disabilities: A national perspective. *Exceptional Children, 59*, 68-76.

Salend, S. J., & Duhaney, L. M. G. (2002). Grading students in inclusive settings. *Teaching Exceptional Children, 34*(3), 8-15.

Schumm, J.S., Vaughn, S., & Harris, J. (1997). Pyramid power for collaborative planning. *Teaching Exceptional Children, 29*(6), 62-66.

Slavin, R. E. (1980). Effects of individual learning expectations on student achievement. *Journal of Educational Psychology, 72*, 520-524.

Stiggins, R.J., Frisbie, D.A., & Griswold, P.A. (1989). Inside high school grading practices: Building a research agenda. *Educational Management: Issues and Practices, 8*(2), 5-14.

Terwilliger, J. S. (1977). Assigning grades—philosophical issues and practical recommendations. *Journal of Research and Development in Education, 10*, 21-39.

Thompson, S. J., Quenemoen, R. F., Thurlow, M. L., & Ysseldyke, J. G. (2001). *Alternate assessments for students with disabilities.* Thousand Oaks, CA: Corwin Press.

Thurlow, M. L. (2002). Positive educational results for all students: The promise of standards-based reform. *Remedial and Special Education, 23*, 195-202.

Valdes, R. A., Williamson, C. L., & Wagner, M. M. (1990). *The national transition study of special education (Vol. 1).* Menlo Park, CA: SRI International.

Welch, A. B. (2000). Responding to student concerns about fairness. *Teaching Exceptional Children, 33*(2), 36-40.

Zobroski, J. (1981). Planning for and grading LD students. *Academic Therapy, 16*(4), 463-473.

Appendix A
Case Study: Tania

Background

Tania is a 7th grader attending Valley Middle School. She receives special education services for a learning disability that affects her reading comprehension, written communication, and organizational skills. Her IEP goals and objectives address her need to improve the ability to summarize what she has read and to answer literal questions following reading. Writing objectives indicate a need to improve paragraph writing and spelling. Tania's IEP does not include a goal addressing organizational skills.

Tania is included in general education content area classes with her peers. Mr. Robinson, the special educator, supports Tania by collaborating with the general education teachers during planning time and suggesting or making modifications to assignments for Tania. Most of Mr. Robinson's support of Tania comes from his individual help during the study period.

Tania is perceived by her teachers to be a hard worker who accepts support when offered. She is somewhat shy and does ask for help in class when her peers are nearby. At the end of the first marking period, Tania receives her report card and takes it home to show her parents. They are disappointed to see the grades of D social studies and F in language arts.

Tania's parents immediately call Mr. Robinson to schedule a meeting to discuss their daughter's performance.

Preparing for the Meeting

At the team meeting the next day, Mr. Robinson initiated a discussion of Tania's grades and the upcoming meeting. The social studies teacher shared her regret that Tania received such a low grade because she was a nice student and worked hard. But her test scores were very low, which makes her report card grade low.

Then each of the general educators discussed the assignments that were most difficult for Tania in their classes, and a consensus was reached that Tania struggled most with tests and quizzes, and on extended assignments such as projects that require her to self-manage her work.

The team of teachers decided that the language arts and social studies teachers would represent the team at the meeting with Tania's parents.

The Initial Meeting

Mr. Robinson acted as the facilitator for the meeting, maintaining an informal and comfortable atmosphere as the group discussed why Tania had received low grades.

In preparation for the meeting, Mr. Robinson reviewed materials he had received at a professional conference on the topic of grading. Included in these materials was information about the personalized grading plans (PGPs). He presented a brief overview and rationale for a personalized grading plan, and the group agreed that a PGP might benefit Tania. They agreed to complete the forms (tools) that Mr. Robinson shared and to reconvene three days later to construct a PGP for Tania.

Preparing for the PGP Meeting

In preparation for the PGP meeting, Tania, her parents, and her teachers completed a survey on what they expected grades to communicate. They also completed a checklist of Tania's strengths and limitations for each class.

A brief, non-technical overview of grading adaptations was distributed to all team members, and Tania's teachers were asked to evaluate each adaptation and select those most appropriate for Tania.

The PGP Meeting

The meeting began with a discussion of the purposes for grades. As team members shared their responses to the survey, it became clear that they all wanted Tania's grades to communicate her effort on her work. But several team members also wanted her grades to reflect progress on individual goals. To complicate matters, Tania's mother and two of her teachers wanted grades to reflect Tania's progress on the general education curriculum.

After an informative discussion, the team reached the following conclusions:

1. Tania's effort would be considered in her grades, but should be only 25% or less of her grade.

2. The best way to measure Tania's progress on individual goals would be to track her progress on IEP objectives.

3. Tania's performance on the regular classroom assignments, with supports described in her IEP, would make up at least 65% of her grade. That way her grades would reflect progress on the general education curriculum.

The Grading Adaptations

Once the team had clarified the purposes for Tania's grades, they moved on to a review of each of the adaptations. Tania's teachers had prioritized adaptations that involve grading effort, grading progress on IEP objectives, and grading process use as potentially helpful for Tania.

The team discussed the pros and cons for each of the adaptations, and agreed to the following adaptations for Tania:

1. **Grading process use**: The team agreed that Tania would receive credit for completing study guides or organizers that were provided to her to prepare for tests in social studies and language arts. Although Tania regularly received study guides before tests and quizzes, she did not always complete them and her teachers usually did not review or correct her work. Now, 10% of Tania's grade on a test or quiz would be based on her completion of the study guide or organizer ahead of time.

2. **Grading process use**: Tania's disability affected her organizational skills, and she had lost points for not completing projects in social studies and language arts. The problem was that Tania would lose her assignment and her work in progress, so that she had little or nothing to turn in on the due date. These problems persisted despite constant reminders form her teachers and parents to maintain her assignment notebook and check due dates for assignments. Now, Tania would receive two grades for each project – a grade based on the quality of the project and a grade based on her completion of a checklist developed at the beginning of the project. Tania's teachers would help her develop the checklist of tasks, and would initial the checklist as she completed the steps in the project.

3. **Grading process on IEP objectives**: Tania's problems with understanding the texts in her classes affected her performance on every assignment. Thus, the team agreed that her progress on reading comprehension was important enough to warrant incorporation into the grading system in social studies and language arts. The social studies, language arts, and special education teachers agreed that all students in the class would receive a worksheet of questions at the end of each section of reading. Tania's performance on the questions would be used to measure her progress in using comprehension strategies, such as outlining and

summarizing and highlighting new vocabulary words and checking their meaning, that she had already used to learn. If Tania was not able to answer the questions correctly, she would receive additional instruction from her teachers.

What about Effort?

After the team had agreed on the above adaptations, they returned to the topic of effort. Tania's parents were the first to say that they felt that the proposed adaptations would be helpful because Tania would put forth her best effort to complete the study guides, checklists, and worksheets. In essence, her effort would be rewarded by more points and probably higher grades.

Tania's teachers agreed that an adaptation involving grading of effort might not be needed because Tania's effort was already high. She didn't need to work harder, she needed to work differently by using the strategies targeted in the grading adaptation.

The team agreed that a monitoring form would be sent home every two weeks for Tania's parents to review, initial, and return. If after a month Tania was not earning points for completing the study guides, checklists, or worksheets, the team would discuss changes to the grading adaptations.

Appendix B
Reproducible Tools

Readers are permitted to duplicate the
materials in Appendix B for non-
commercial classroom use. Any other
uses require written permission from
the publisher.

Tool 3-1
Survey of Grading Purposes: Parent Version, Part 1

Instructions: Rank the 12 purposes in order of importance by writing a number 1-12 next to each purpose (1= most important, 12 = least important). Use each number only once.

Purposes for Grades   Ranking

1. Tell me whether my child has improved in his/her classes.   Rank___

2. Tell me how to help my child plan for his/her future.   Rank___

3. Tell me how hard my child is trying.   Rank___

4. Tell me what my child needs to improve on to keep a good grade. Rank___

5. Tell me how well my child works with classmates.   Rank___

6. Tell me what my child is good at and not so good at.   Rank___

7. Tell colleges and employers what my child is good at.   Rank___

8. Tell me how much my child can do on his/her own.   Rank___

9. Tell me how my child's performance compares to other children.   Rank___

10. Tell me how much of the general curriculum my child mastered.   Rank___

11. Tell me what classes my child should take in high school.   Rank___

12. Motivate my child to try harder.   Rank___

Tool 3-1
Survey of Grading Purposes: Parent Version, Part 2

Instructions: Transfer your rankings from Part 1 to the interpretive chart in Part 2. Sum the ranks for the items in each Focus Area. The lower the score, the more important that Focus Area is perceived.

Focus Area: Academic Performance

Item	Ranking
1. Tell me whether my child has improved in his/her classes.	_____
9. Tell me how my child's performance compares to other children.	_____
10. Tell me how much of the general curriculum my child mastered.	_____
8. Tell me how much my child can do on his/her own.	_____
Total	_____

Focus Area: Affective and Behavioral

Item	Ranking
5. Tell me how well my child works with classmates.	_____
3. Tell me how hard my child is trying.	_____
12. Motivate my child to try harder.	_____
4. Tell me what my child needs to improve on to keep a good grade.	_____
Total	_____

Focus Area: Transition and Postsecondary Planning

Item	Ranking
2. Tell me how to help my child plan for his/her future.	_____
11. Tell me what classes my child should take in high school.	_____
7. Tell colleges and employers what my child is good at.	_____
6. Tell me what my child is good at and not so good at.	_____
Total	_____

Tool 6-1
Clarifying Prioritized Content and How It Will Be Assessed

Prioritized Content	Expectation Areas in Which Primarily Assessed for Grading
Most Important	Check all that apply
	____ classwork ____ homework ____ projects ____ groupwork ____ tests/quizzes
	____ classwork ____ homework ____ projects ____ groupwork ____ tests/quizzes
	____ classwork ____ homework ____ projects ____ groupwork ____ tests/quizzes
	____ classwork ____ homework ____ projects ____ groupwork ____ tests/quizzes
	____ classwork ____ homework ____ projects ____ groupwork ____ tests/quizzes
	____ classwork ____ homework ____ projects ____ groupwork ____ tests/quizzes

Tool 6-2
Prioritizing Content in Your Scope and Sequence Chart for a Marking Period

Ranked Content		Areas of Expectation
1.		- classwork - homework - group work - test/quiz - project
2.		- classwork - homework - group work - test/quiz - project
3.		- classwork - homework - group work - test/quiz - project
4.		- classwork - homework - group work - test/quiz - project
5.		- classwork - homework - group work - test/quiz - project
6.		- classwork - homework - group work - test/quiz - project

Tool 7-1
Analyzing Processes in Assignments

Students with disabilities may have difficulty with processes that most typical students complete effortlessly. Also, students with disabilities may have to learn to use different processes that help them overcome the effects of their disability. It is important that general and special educators collaborate to identify the processes embedded in an assignment, and to pinpoint processes that a student with a disability may need to use in order to complete the assignment.

Example: Five-Paragraph Essay

Steps to Complete Assignment	Processes Most Students Use	What an Individual Student Needs to Do	Related IEP Objective	Type of Process
1. Brainstorm a topic	Dialogue with a peer or teacher	Develop timeline for entire assignment		___ learning strategy ___ assistive technology _X_ self-management strategy
2. Create a graphic organizer using the topic	Work with teacher to identify important components of topic on graphic organizer supplied by the teacher	Electronic speller / dictionary / thesaurus		___ learning strategy ___ assistive technology _X_ self-management strategy
3. Outline five paragraphs	Follow format provided by the teacher			___ learning strategy ___ assistive technology _X_ self-management strategy

Tool 7-1 continued

Steps to Complete Assignment	Processes Most Students Use	What an Individual Student Needs to Do	Related IEP Objective	Type of Process
4. Write rough draft	Use outline and word processor to write rough draft	Use word processor with word prediction		___ learning strategy _X_ assistive technology ___ self-management strategy
5. Edit rough draft	Use editing checklist provided by the teacher. Submit product for peer review			___ learning strategy ___ assistive technology _X_ self-management strategy
6. Write final draft (publish)	Make necessary changes using the word processor			___ learning strategy ___ assistive technology _X_ self-management strategy

Tool 7-2
Evaluating Processes to Be Incorporated into the Grading Process

Processes	Criteria
List the processes you found when analyzing an assignment.	
1.	- very important for completing work in this class - very important for completing future work - grading process may motivate student - very important for increasing student independence
2.	- very important for completing work in this class - very important for completing future work - grading process may motivate student - very important for increasing student independence
3.	- very important for completing work in this class - very important for completing future work - grading process may motivate student - very important for increasing student independence
4.	- very important for completing work in this class - very important for completing future work - grading process may motivate student - very important for increasing student independence
List the processes that are described in the student's IEP objectives	
1.	- very important for completing work in this class - very important for completing future work - grading process may motivate student - very important for increasing student independence
2.	- very important for completing work in this class - very important for completing future work - grading process may motivate student - very important for increasing student independence
3.	- very important for completing work in this class - very important for completing future work - grading process may motivate student - very important for increasing student independence

Tool 7-2 continued

Processes	Criteria
List the process that the student must use to take advantage of accommodations	
1.	- very important for completing work in this class - very important for completing future work - grading process may motivate student - very important for increasing student independence
2.	- very important for completing work in this class - very important for completing future work - grading process may motivate student - very important for increasing student independence
3.	- very important for completing work in this class - very important for completing future work - grading process may motivate student - very important for increasing student independence
4.	- very important for completing work in this class - very important for completing future work - grading process may motivate student - very important for increasing student independence
5.	- very important for completing work in this class - very important for completing future work - grading process may motivate student - very important for increasing student independence
6.	- very important for completing work in this class - very important for completing future work - grading process may motivate student - very important for increasing student independence

Tool 8-1
Evaluating IEP Objectives for Grading on Progress Adaptation

IEP Objectives	How will progress directly affect performance in class curriculum?	How will progress increase independent functioning?	Is significant emphasis placed on work addressing this objective?	How will progress increase access to general education curriculum?	Can objective be addressed regularly in general education class?	Comments
1.						
2.						
3.						
4.						
5.						

Tool 8-2
Preparing IEP Objectives for Grading

IEP Objective	Dimension for Measuring	How Progress Will be Measured	How Progress Will Be Monitored	How Progress Will Be Translated to Grade	Incorporating into Grade
	- accuracy - rate - frequency - level of support - rubric score - other (specify)	-percentages for accuracy - rate - level of independence - total frequency -met/unmet - rubric score - other (specify)	__ same assignments as rest of class __ special probes given on a schedule to the student __ assignments modified to provide work on the objective	- convert percentages to grades - convert total frequences to grade - convert mean rate to grade - convert met/unmet to grade - convert total rubric scores - other (specify)	- separate grade - multiple grade - part of grade in other area

Tool 9-1
Pinpointing Areas in Which to Grade Improvement

Performance Area	Specific Assignment	Measure of Improvement	Converting Improvement to Grade
Classwork		___ higher score or points ___ occur more often ___ higher percentages ___ increased accuracy ___ other	
Homework		___ higher score or points ___ occur more often ___ higher percentages ___ increased accuracy ___ other	
Groupwork		___ higher score or points ___ occur more often ___ higher percentages ___ increased accuracy ___ other	
Test/Quiz		___ higher score or points ___ occur more often ___ higher percentages ___ increased accuracy ___ other	
Project		___ higher score or points ___ occur more often ___ higher percentages ___ increased accuracy ___ other	
Other		___ higher score or points ___ occur more often ___ higher percentages ___ increased accuracy ___ other	

Tool 10-1
Changing Your Grading Scale or Weights

Current Grading Scales	Proposed Grading Scale	Rationale
Daily Assignments		
Report Cards		

Current Weights for Report Cards	Proposed Weights	Rationale
Classwork =		
Homework =		
Tests/Quizzes =		
Groupwork =		
Projects =		
Rules/Expectations =		
Other =		

Index

-S-

social promotion 4, 125

standards-based reform 4, 70

-T-

teacher preparation concerning grading 13

technology support of IEP goals 82-84

-Z-

zero as a grade 138